Out of Formation

Spiritual Disciplines,
of God and Men

Dr. Gary E. Gilley

EP BOOKS

Faverdale North

Darlington

DL3 0PH, England

www.epbooks.org

sales@epbooks.org

EP BOOKS are distributed in the USA by:

JPL Fulfillment

3741 Linden Avenue Southeast,

Grand Rapids, MI 49548.

E-mail: sales@jplfulfillment.com

Tel: 877.683.6935

First published 2014

British Library Cataloguing in Publication Data available

ISBN 978-1-78397-041-4

"What is today a matter of academic speculation begins tomorrow to move armies and pull down empires."

—J. Gresham Machen

This book is dedicated to those who have worked behind the scenes to make my writing ministry possible: Pat Lane (who read an article of mine and knew I desperately needed a proofreader), Linda Kestner ("Think on These Things" administrative assistant), Bev Byerline (Southern View Chapel's administrative assistant), Marsha Gilley (my loving wife) and numerous others (you know who you are).

Contents

Introduction

The Spiritual Formation Movement, sometimes referred to as "the spiritual disciples" or simply "Christian spirituality," is radically changing the church. Ancient disciplines, most often practiced within the monastic movement in the early centuries of Christianity, have been dusted off, repacked, and resubmitted to believers as the means whereby spiritual growth is obtained. There is increasing discussion about fasting, journaling, pilgrimage, simplicity, solitude, silence, contemplative prayer, and spiritual direction in Christian literature. What can be learned from this renewed interest in spiritual formation, and what are the dangers? Part One of this volume has been written to interact with the history, teachings and dangers of the Spiritual Formation Movement. Part Two will turn to the biblical alternatives for spiritual formation, as described in Part One.

There we will examine the means, or disciplines if you choose, which the Word of God clearly identify as ways God has designed for His people to be transformed into Christ-likeness, and to experience intimacy with Him.

As will be seen in the first section of this book, the modern Spiritual Formation Movement is a reintroduction of ancient extra-biblical practices created and developed by members of the early church. These practices, often called disciplines, promised to enable the users to grow closer to the Lord, experience divine communion and hear the voice of God. While these disciplines did not emerge directly from Scripture, many had a loose connection which enabled the originators to claim a biblical base for their practices. Other disciplines have no scriptural foundation at all, rather they appear via supposed visions, dreams and revelations from God. As time moved on these disciplines multiplied, and became acceptable within certain segments of Christianity.

Practiced and defined increasingly by hermits, monks and within monastic communities, such disciplines became associated with "holy" men and women—the spiritual elite. While the average church member was vaguely aware of some of these supposed marks of holiness, most were ignorant of how the system worked. Super-holiness, it would seem, was for a unique class of Christians; few others had the time or inclination for spiritual formation. Thus, spiritual disciplines stayed primarily within the narrow bounds of monasteries and the like for centuries. There were apparently some attempts to broaden their appeal, as is evidenced by the use of a little 14th century book, of questionable authorship, *The Cloud of Unknowing*. But it would not be until the 1970s that the spiritual disciplines would break free of their obscurity and become exposed to a wider audience. When this took place the disciplines moved quickly from their Roman Catholic and Orthodox roots to infiltrate Protestant and evangelical circles as well. To many evangelicals it was as if the lights had come on. Suddenly a whole spiritual world had been revealed to those hungry for something fresh, something real, something personal that they were not experiencing with God. For such people the Spiritual Formation Movement hit the spot. As taught by Richard Foster and Dallas Willard, and promoted by ministries such as Foster's Renovaré and Youth Specialties, spiritual formation gradually became a major voice within evangelicalism. Today the Spiritual Formation Movement not only continues its rapid growth but has become readily accepted as a means of discipleship. Most Bible colleges and seminaries now have spiritual formation departments and offer related degrees. Rare is an evangelical author who does not quote from the Christian mystics and/or recommends some of these ancient practices as fresh means of spiritual growth.

And for many the disciplines seem to work. Testimonies can be multiplied by adherents as to their renewed passion for God, their experience of divine intimacy, and their spiritual development. But as always, pragmatism, testimonies and experience cannot direct us in the search for truth; only the Word of God can be our authoritative guide. With this in mind it is vital that we take the Spiritual Formation Movement through the grid of Scripture to determine its place in the life of the follower of Jesus Christ. We will find that many of these disciplines, as defined and practiced within the movement, lack biblical support. They are the ideas of men and women, not the doctrines of God. As such many of these practices should be abandoned as the believer turns with conviction to the true disciplines given to us by the Lord Himself.

The modern Spiritual Formation Movement has been in existence for almost 40 years and shows no signs of fading away. Unlike the numerous fads that rush through evangelicalism, lasting a year or two and then being trashed to make way for the next wave, spiritual formation seems to be here to stay. It has of course morphed, matured and changed in many ways throughout the years, but at this time it seems to be gaining momentum and influence. This is due in large part to a number of factors:

- Renovaré: This is Richard Foster's organization founded in 1988 to promote spiritual formation throughout the globe. Foster himself has written many books and articles, as has his mentor Dallas Willard, which have been well received by all branches of Christianity. Renovaré has published *The Renovaré Spiritual Formation Study Bible*, since renamed *The Life with God Bible*. As would be expected this study Bible is highly ecumenical, drawing its study notes from a wide variety of Christian traditions including Catholicism, Orthodoxy and Quakerism. And of course, the study notes promote a mystical approach to the Christian life.

• Seminaries: Most seminaries, and many Bible colleges, now have a department of spiritual formation and are offering degrees in the disciplines. Biola University, and its Talbot School of Theology is representative of many relatively conservative Christian schools of higher education that have bought into spiritual formation and is spreading its message. Talbot offers an MA and M.Div in Spiritual Formation and Soul Care. They boast on their website, "Since we began offering spiritual direction, hundreds upon hundreds of people have experienced either individual or group spiritual direction through the ministry of the Center for Spiritual Renewal." As Bible colleges and seminaries train the next generation of pastors, missionaries and Christian leaders we can expect that spiritual formation will continue to gain traction in the evangelical community.

• Publishing houses: Prior to the publication of Foster's *Celebration of Discipline* in 1978 virtually all spiritual and mystical literature was produced by Catholic and

Orthodox publishing houses such as Paulist Press or the Jesuits. Not anymore as evangelical publishers are rushing to get to press these bestselling books and authors. NavPress, InterVarsity, Thomas Nelson and a host of others have entered the market. Christians, who had grown accustomed to trusting these publishing houses, are being caught off-guard by what they are reading from them today.

- Authors/books/magazines: As the publishing houses are looking to cash in on the interest in spiritual formation, authors by the score have stepped up to meet the demand. In addition, there are an abundance of evangelical magazines such as *Christianity Today* (which is highly sympathetic and a strong promoter of spiritual formation authors and their literature).

- Emerging and Seeker churches: It cannot be denied that emerging churches and ministries are on the cutting edge. As movements that have reflected their culture more than Scripture, their leaders are constantly on the watch for shifts in interest and taste in the world around them. Seeker churches originally targeted the baby boomers who apparently wanted to go to church and not feel like they had been to church. Anything that would make them uncomfortable was eliminated and the church took on a secular persona. But the younger emerging demographic seems to desire a sense of the sacred. To accommodate this group the emerging and seeker leaders have turned to spiritual formation with its ancient spiritual practices that promise intimacy with God. This younger crowd, many of which not been trained in theological thinking or biblical discernment, is easily deceived by the rhetoric and methods of spiritual formation.

For these reasons, and perhaps several more, I do not see any diminishing of the influence of spiritual formation on the church in the decades to come. This is certainly one of the greatest threats facing biblical Christianity today. May the Lord raise up a generation that will return to the Sacred Text and stand once again on *Sola Scriptura*. It is my hope and prayer that this little volume will shed light on the Spiritual Formation Movement and draw the readers back to the firm foundation of biblical truth.

14

Part One
The Spiritual Formation Movement

1

Spiritual Formation

Almost everyone on the cutting edge of Christianity is talking about spiritual formation. From books to magazine articles to sermons to seminary courses, spiritual formation is a hot topic. What is spiritual formation? What does it teach? Is it something to embrace, ignore or fight? In the pages to follow I want to examine some of these questions and more, devoting careful attention to detailing and evaluating aspects of what has been called the "Spiritual Formation Movement." In this first chapter I intend to offer a definition of spiritual formation, trace its origins, mention a few of its practices, illustrate its recent popularity, and briefly identify its strengths and dangers.

In Search of a Definition

When the average person speaks of spiritual formation they assume that it is a modern or trendy synonym for discipleship. Throughout church history, in obedience to the Lord's command found in the Great Commission (Matthew 28:19–20), the church has dedicated itself to the task of making disciples, or followers of Jesus Christ. Perhaps growing weary of using the same word all the time, some more creative people have substituted other words such as mentoring, although that word is taken out of a secular context rather than a biblical one. Mentoring usually implies a one-on-one effort in which a more mature Christian is training a less mature believer as in, "I was mentored by Joe." I think the word mentoring, simply because of its implications, common use, and background, is not the best word to describe what Scripture calls "making disciples." When we examine the New Testament we find that disciple-making is not the prerogative of individuals only, but also of the church. That is, disciples are made not by one-on-one relationships so much as by the ministry of the fuller body of Christ. While we can all point to special people in our lives who have been instrumental in our spiritual growth, and while we should all be actively involved on some level in discipling others, and while most dedicate their discipling efforts to a few people, potential disciples need the balance of the wider membership of the church to become the followers of Christ that the Lord intends (Ephesians 4:11–16; 1 Corinthians 12). It is best, it seems to me, to stay with the biblical terminology which serves us well in understanding the task before us.

While the term "mentoring" is still used by some, it would appear that "spiritual formation" has supplanted both it and "discipleship" in the vocabulary of many. However, spiritual formation is not equivalent to discipleship, or mentoring for that matter. Some trace the roots of the Spiritual Formation Movement to 1974 when Father William Menninger, a Trappist monk, found an ancient book entitled *The Cloud of Unknowing* in the library at St. Joseph's Abbey in Spencer, Massachusetts. This 14th century book offered a means by which contemplative practices, long used by Catholic monks, could be taught to lay people. As Menninger began teaching these contemplative practices, his abbot, Thomas Keating, along with Basil Pennington, another Trappist monk, began to spread the concepts Menninger was teaching.[1] But it was Richard Foster's 1978 book, *Celebration of Discipline*, that launched the popularity and present interest in spiritual formation. It was by this landmark book, described by *Christianity Today* as one of the ten best books of the 20th century, that Catholic and Eastern Orthodox disciplines, practiced by the Desert Fathers and Mothers[2] as well as monks and hermits, were introduced to evangelicalism. These disciplines were not completely unknown to evangelicals who were familiar with church history, but they were now being repackaged and offered as a means of spiritual growth and maturity. In fact, the implication was that without the use of these ancient contemplative methods true "spiritual formation" was not possible. Long accepted biblical disciplines, such as Bible study and prayer, were framed as quaint and simplistic. Worse, believers were told that these biblical disciplines were forged from a Western "worldview of the head." If the believer wanted to move deeply into the things of God, such practices were not enough, for they never really reach the heart, leaving the unsuspecting Christian with little more than a superficial intellectual knowledge of the divine with no depth. Bruce Demarest, long time Professor of Christian Theology and Spiritual Formation at Denver Seminary states, "The heart discovers and experiences God; reason demonstrates and explains God."[3] The same author quotes Brennan Manning as saying, "The engaged mind, illumined by truth, awakens awareness; the engaged heart, affected by love, awakens passion."[4] The rather explicit implication throughout spiritual formation literature is that Bible study feeds the head, but if one wants to feed the heart they must turn to the spiritual disciplines.

As more and more authors, teachers, publishers and schools began to echo the same refrain evangelicals became intimidated. They did not want to be left out of the newest, and supposedly best, means of discipleship and so they began to read and listen to these new contemplative teachers. As they did so they found that almost every spiritual formation book and sermon opened by tapping into the innate dissatisfaction that all believers recognize. It goes something like this: "Are you not tired of the Christian life you have been living? Haven't you grown weary of reading the Bible, praying, and going to church? Wouldn't you really like to enter into the very depth of your soul and encounter God in indescribable experiences that will radically change you forever? If so, then you must learn and live out the disciplines that have been used by the historic church almost since its inception. Read this book (or take this course or go to this renewal retreat or work on this degree, etc.) and we will teach you what the spiritual masters of the past knew but that we have long forgotten."

On the basis of such promises the modern Spiritual Formation Movement was birthed and now flourishes. It sometimes goes by different handles such as Contemplative Spirituality or simply the Spiritual Disciplines, but they all refer to the same thing. Bruce Demarest offers this definition in his book *Satisfy Your Soul*, "Spiritual formation is an ancient ministry of the church, concerned with the 'forming' or 'shaping' of a believer's character and actions into the likeness of Christ."[5] Richard Foster would agree, "Christian spiritual formation is a God-ordained process that shapes our entire person so that we take on the character and being of Christ himself."[6] This sounds much like the definition of discipleship as found in Scripture, but before we relax let's return to Professor Demarest, who tells us that spiritual formation is not only concerned with orthodox doctrine but with "many practices that open [us] up to the presence and direction of God."[7] This rather benign comment actually unlocks the door to the Spiritual Formation Movement and how it differs from biblical discipleship. *What distinguishes spiritual formation from discipleship is not in its basically similar definition, but its source, its practices, and its philosophy.*

Source

Perhaps one of the most important factors to understand when analyzing spiritual formation is its source or origin. Its teachers are fond of stating that their disciplines have old roots, going back to the earliest days of the church. Dan Kimble, in his book *The Emerging Church*, calls this the vintage church, while Robert Webber, author of *Ancient-Future Faith*, refers to it as the classic stage of church history (approximately the second through the sixth century). Such men have grown tired of superficial church life that has dominated much of Christianity since the insurgence of the "seeker-friendly" model. They desire something with more substance and more historical connection than what the modern church experience offers. They suggest we study the past and pattern our lives and churches after the rich and vibrant spiritual dynamics that we supposedly find there.

I believe these men almost get it right—almost. In fact, we do need to look to the past to see how we should live and function in the present. The problem is that the spiritual formation leaders do not go back far enough. In their march into the past they stop at the classical or vintage age of church formation instead of returning to the New Testament Scriptures. This is the fatal flaw in the whole movement. The early church (post-apostolic, not New Testament church) did many things right and many things wrong. Its pronouncements, views, rituals, organizations, and structures can be examined with profit, but they were not without error. I recently taught a course on the history of Christian doctrine using as a textbook John Hannah's excellent book *Our Legacy*. In that course of study I found it most discouraging to discover how very quickly the early church departed from the teaching of the epistles. Both doctrinally and ecclesiastically the church, during the "classical" stage, moved beyond the inspired Word of God to establish its own views, doctrines, philosophies, rituals and formats.

On a doctrinal level all one has to do is read a few pages in the highly acclaimed (by those who promote spiritual formation) *Ancient Christian Commentary on Scripture* series. This 27-volume set (including the Apocrypha) is designed to enlighten this generation concerning the views of the early church fathers and theologians. The need for such a series is stated in the flyleaf of each volume, "Today the historical-critical method of interpretation has nearly exhausted its claim on the biblical text and on the church. In its wake there is a widespread yearning among Christian individuals and communities for the wholesome, the deep and the enduring." In other words, it is time to abandon the historical-grammatical hermeneutical method and return to the fanciful and allegorical methods of the early church fathers. When you read the interpretations found in these volumes, you begin to wonder if some of the early church fathers are even reading the same Bible. Many (not all, of course) of the comments on the various texts are so whimsical and imaginative that any hope of a normal understanding of Scripture is lost. What this commentary series demonstrates very well is why and how the church went astray early in its history. When you twist Scripture to mean anything you want it to mean, where you end up can be quite bizarre.

A good example of what emerged from this type of hermeneutic is the monastic movement in which the so-called Desert Fathers and Mothers migrated to the Egyptian wilderness to live as hermits and supposedly contemplate God. In misguided zeal (and without direction from Scripture) these men and women would often starve themselves, expose their bodies to the elements, go as long as possible without sleep and live isolated from civilization. Under these peculiar and extreme conditions many of them claimed to have visions and encounters with the Lord that normal Christians did not have. As a result, some declared these individuals super-saints and their visions and dreams as revelatory words from the Lord. They were elevated to the status of Christian celebrities. These are the very ones that Richard Foster, Dallas Willard, and Bruce Demarest call "spiritual masters" and from whom they draw their understanding of spiritual formation. As we will see time and time again, the teachings, methods, and concepts behind the Spiritual Formation Movement are drawn from these early contemplative hermits, as well as the medieval monks and nuns, principally from the Counter-Reformation period, not from Scripture.

It is absolutely essential to get this connection early in our study. Many, if not most, of the disciplines and instructions found within spiritual formation are not drawn from Scripture; they are drawn from the imaginations of men and women passed along through tradition. Demarest tells his readers that for help in spiritual formation we are to "turn to our Christian past—to men and women who understood how the soul finds satisfaction as we grow in God, and how His Spirit finds a more ready home in us."[8] And just who are these people to whom we are supposed to turn?" Demarest suggests John of the Cross, Henri Nouwen, Francis of Assisi, Teresa of Ávila, the desert fathers and mothers, and the Christians mystics.[9] Other highly touted mystics include Thomas Keating, Thomas Merton, Francis De Sales, Thomas Kelly, Madame Guyon, Theophan the Recluse, Ignatius of Loyola, Meister Eckhart, and Julian of Norwich. Virtually every author who has written a book on spiritual formation draws his or her understanding of the Christian life, and especially Christian experiences, from this stable of mystics. In other words, spiritual formation is not founded on the New Testament Scriptures but mostly on the experiences of Roman Catholic mystics, with a few Eastern Orthodox and

Quakers thrown into the mix. This is important to understand from the beginning of our study, so I will repeat: the Spiritual Formation Movement is not based on Scripture but on the experiences, writings, and imaginations of those who teach a false gospel and misunderstand the Christian life as detailed in God's Word.

With this in mind, we need to turn to the practices deemed absolutely essential by the mystics for spiritual formation. These are usually termed spiritual disciplines. What disciplines are we talking about?

Disciplines

John Ortberg, a former teaching pastor at Willow Creek Community Church, describes spiritual disciplines as "any activity that can help me gain power to live life as Jesus taught and modeled it. How many spiritual disciplines are there? As many as we can think of."[10] Is this the case? Can virtually any activity be turned into a spiritual discipline? Does God sanction all spiritual practices and endorse them as means of progressive sanctification? Biblical disciplines, which are indispensable for spiritual growth and discipleship, are, of course, positive things. But man-made disciplines are at best optional and are certainly not essential for spiritual growth, or else God's Word would have commanded them and provided instruction for their use. Scripture clearly speaks of the discipline of Bible study (John 17:17; Psalm 1; Psalm 19; 2 Timothy 3:15–4:6) as necessary for sanctification.

Likewise prayer is mentioned as being a source of spiritual development (Hebrews 4:15–16). And the need for the body of Christ, both in the teaching of truth and mutual ministry (Ephesians 4:11–16; Hebrews 10:24–25), can be clearly found. But when we stray much beyond these we run into trouble. Nevertheless, the Spiritual Formation Movement offers long lists of disciplines that are essential for spiritual development.

Foster, in his *Celebration of Discipline,* provides a chapter each on the following disciplines: meditation, [contemplative] prayer, fasting, study, simplicity, solitude, submission, service, confession, worship, guidance, and celebration. InterVarsity Press has a line of books it calls *Formatio* which offers individual books designed to teach each of the above disciplines plus the sacramental life, silence, journaling, spiritual mentoring, pilgrimage, Sabbath keeping, sacred reading (*lectio divina*), and the need for spiritual directors. Thomas Nelson Publishing has recently published an 8-volume set they call "The Ancient Practices Series." The first book, written by Brian McLaren (which ought to tell the discerning reader something), is *Finding Our Way Again: The Return of the Ancient Practices.* The other books in the series are: *In Constant Prayer, Sabbath, Fasting, Sacred Meal, Sacred Journey, The Liturgical Year and Tithing,* all teaching spiritual disciplines derived from the mystics rather than from the New Testament. NavPress offers its "Spiritual Formation Line" to promote the spiritual disciplines. Many other major Christian publishers are following suit including Zondervan,

which links with Youth Specialties to offer books aimed
toward teaching young people and adults the contemplative
life. Even from the pens of more conservative authors it is
almost rare to read a recently published book that does not
quote at least a few mystics. Some of the more prominent
authors in the field include: Richard Foster (of course), Dallas
Willard, Phyllis Tickle, Robert Benson, Dan Allender, Scot
McKnight, Nora Gallagher, Adele Calhoun, David deSilva,
Ruth Barton, Jan Johnson, Lynne Baab, Diana Butler Bass,
Helen Cepero, Leighton Ford, Larry Crabb, Calvin Miller,
Tricia McCary Rhodes, Mindy Caliguire, Albert Haase,
Eugene Peterson, M. Robert Mulholland Jr., Gordon Smith,
Brian McLaren, John Ortberg, Mark Yaconelli, Brennan
Manning, Bruce Demarest, and Kenneth Boa. And this
might be barely scratching the surface.

Future chapters will directly address and critique many
of these disciplines but for now it is important to note that
Scripture does not teach that any of these (as defined in
most spiritual formation literature) are a means of spiritual
growth, sanctification or discipleship. Some of the spiritual
disciplines encouraged are mentioned in the Word, yet very
little specific detail is given on how they are to be observed
or their purpose. Take fasting for example. Every reader of
Scripture knows that fasting is mentioned on numerous
occasions, but few comprehend its purpose and function.
At no point in the Bible are we told that fasting enhances
spiritual growth, or produces spiritual formation, although it

has spiritual implications (we will look specifically at fasting in a future chapter).

If the spiritual disciplines, as are being taught by the leaders of the Spiritual Formation Movement, are not actually found in Scripture, how can Christian authors be so assertive in recommending them? They often do so because they are convinced that the human authors of Scripture were strong practitioners of the spiritual disciplines, but the disciplines were so much a part of first century life that the inspired authors saw no need to mention them in the New Testament. Dallas Willard, the "mentor" of Richard Foster, writes that Paul, for example, lived out the spiritual disciplines but did not write about them in the epistles for, "Obviously ... for him and the readers of his own day, [there would be] no need to write a book on the disciplines for the spiritual life that explained systematically what he had in mind ... But quite a bit of time has passed—and many abuses have occurred in the name of spiritual disciplines [since that time]."[11]

What Willard is saying is that the only reason Paul and the apostles did not write about the disciplines is because they were already being practiced and modeled by the apostles to such an extent that no one at the time needed more information and insight into them. This is of course not only an argument from silence but a bit ludicrous as well. Did not the believers see Paul modeling prayer, preaching, body life and the study of Scripture? If so, why did he bother to write about the importance of these while completely ignoring many of the disciplines about which spiritual formation leaders are excited? The answer to this question is of extreme importance. Willard believes that, if Christians today are to live as the apostles and early disciples did, it is important that they somehow share in their experience but since, of course, we do not live with them, all we can do is read about their lives. This leaves us alienated from the lives of early disciples and therefore lacking in their spirituality. What can we do? "The only way to overcome this alienation from their sort of life," Willard suggests, "is by entering into the actual practices of Jesus and Paul as something essential to our life in Christ."[12] By this he means that we must engage in the spiritual disciplines that he *assumes* the early believers practiced (although we are never told so in the New Testament, nor mandated to do so).

This leads us to a fork in the road early in our studies. Do we, as believers in *sola Scriptura*, take our marching orders from the written Word, or do we look to the "white spaces" in Scripture to determine how we live? Do we actually believe that the Lord has given us in Scripture the teachings and practices He wants us to follow, or do we believe that we must supplement the authentic words of God with our imagination and traditions of men? This is increasingly becoming an issue within almost all branches of evangelicalism. Once it is accepted that we can enhance the Christian life by augmenting the inspired words of Scripture there is no limit to where we might end up. Take Bruce Demarest for example. As a long time conservative professor at a strong evangelical seminary, when he was first exposed to spiritual formation he resisted but in time he claimed he got over his biases and accepted the teachings behind it. He writes, "Admittedly I found that certain beliefs and traditions remained foreign to me, being based more on tradition than solidly on Scripture. All denominations have their blind spots. But I also found that, once I got past my old prejudices and misunderstanding, I accepted more than I rejected."[3]

Philosophy

The Spiritual Formation Movement is concerned more about individual experience than biblical knowledge or truth. This does not mean that adherents are totally uninterested in the Bible, and some would know it well. But the emphasis is on what a person experiences through the Bible more so than what they learn. Contemplatives, such as Dallas Willard and Richard Foster, will strongly encourage Bible reading and prayer but they mean something different from what most Christians mean when they reference the same terms. As we will see in future chapters, contemplative prayer is not the same as prayer defined biblically; "sacred reading" (also called *lectio divina*) of Scripture is not the same as Bible study; meditation (mystically encountering God) is not the same as knowing God and so forth. Many of the same terms are used, but as the classical liberals, and the more recent emergents, are fond of doing, they take our terms, including biblical ones, and give them new definitions and twists.

Many of the spiritual disciplines that are supposedly necessary for spiritual formation are either not found in the Bible, or have been redefined to mean something foreign to the scriptural meaning. We are being told that disciplines such as silence, journaling, or observing the liturgical calendar will transform our lives even though God's Word does not advocate these things as means of spiritual growth. This puts the sincere Christian on the horns of a dilemma: Does Scripture actually "equip [the believer] for every good work" (2 Timothy 3:17) as it promises, or does it not? If the Word is in need of being supplemented by the traditions, practices, and methods of people, which ones are we to choose—and, more importantly, how would we know which ones would be helpful? Do we determine such things by looking to the past and decreeing a particular set of hermits or mystics, who claimed visions and dreams and supernatural encounters with God, as our guide? And if so, which of the mystics get the nod as "spiritual masters" since many of their claims were mutually contradictory and highly fanciful? Or perhaps we should look to pragmatism as our guide. In other words, if it works for you then go for it. This seems to be the collective wisdom of spiritual formation teachers—if it works it must be from God, even if not sanctioned in Scripture.

There are at least two ways spiritual formation leaders

attempt to establish a biblical foundation for the disciplines.
The first has already been alluded to: ancient people were
already practicing disciplines and so direct revelation from
God was not necessary. Willard writes,

> Thoughtful and religiously devout people of the classical
> and Hellenistic world, from the Ganges to the Tiber, knew
> that the mind and body of the human being had to be
> rigorously disciplined to achieve a decent individual and social
> existence. This is not something St. Paul had to prove or even
> explicitly state to his readers—but it also was not something
> he overlooked, leaving it to be thought up by crazed monks in
> the Dark Ages. It is, rather, a wisdom gleaned from millennia of
> collective human experience.[14]

In other words, the wisdom of collective human experience
has recognized the need for religious disciplines, therefore a
word from the Lord was unnecessary in biblical times. But
the reality is that "collective human experience" and wisdom,
especially in regard to religion, is self-deceiving (Proverbs
14:12). Man cannot comprehend God apart from divine
revelation. The wisdom of collective human experience has
resulted in every sort of human-created religion, all of which
ultimately lead people astray. The wisdom of man never
draws people to God or His ways (James 3:13–18). This was
one of the key reasons that Jesus Christ came to earth; it was
necessary for Him to "explain" God to us, otherwise we could
never understand Him (John 1:18).

This takes us directly to the second way spiritual formation leaders attempt to lay a biblical foundation for what they teach. They make the claim that spiritual disciplines were practiced by Jesus and the apostles followed suit, therefore we are to do the same thing. Willard tells us, "The key to understanding Paul is to know that ... he lived and practiced daily the things his Lord taught and practiced ... Paul followed Jesus by living as he lived. And how did he do that? Through activities and ways of living that would train his whole personality to depend upon the risen Christ as Christ trained himself to depend upon the Father."[15] What kind of practices does Willard have in mind? Here is a sample, "It is solitude *and solitude alone that opens the possibility of a radical relationship to God* that can withstand all external events up to and beyond death."[16] None of us would deny that Jesus went away on occasion to pray or rest, as did Paul and the other apostles. Nor would any doubt the benefit of spending time alone with the Lord. But when we are told that "it is solitude and solitude alone that opens the possibility of a radical relationship to God," I think it would be nice to have at least one proof text that actually says this. Where in Scripture does God make such a statement? One of the problems facing the evangelical church today is that too many men and women are setting themselves up as the final authority on the Christian life. We need to remember that no matter how famous, successful or popular Christian leaders may become, their authority rests solely on the revealed Word of God, not their own personality or intellect.

One of the points that spiritual formation adherents miss is that the New Testament does address their approach to spirituality. In Colossians 2:20–23 Paul clearly tells us that many of the disciplines that were being promoted then, as well as today, have no spiritual value at all. He asks the Colossians, "Why do you submit yourselves to decrees, such as, 'Do not handle, do not taste, do not touch!' (which all refer to things destined to perish with the using)—in accordance with the commandments and teachings of men? These are matters which have to be sure, the appearance of wisdom in self-made religion and self-abasement and severe treatment of the body, but are of no value against fleshly indulgence."

The essence of the Spiritual Formation Movement is that through the use of their recommended disciplines our fleshly nature will be tamed and we will grow to become like Christ. Willard writes, "[Paul's] crucifixion of the flesh, and ours, is accomplished through those activities such as solitude, fasting, frugality, service, and so forth, which constitute the curriculum in the school of self-denial and place us on the front line of spiritual combat."[17] But the inspired apostle says the exact opposite. Bodily discipline does not control "fleshly indulgence." Victory over sin and spiritual growth is the work (fruit) of the Holy Spirit (Galatians 5:16–26) which is cultivated when we make use of the means that Scripture specifically prescribes, not the practices that have been invented or distorted by men.

Strengths and Dangers

On the positive side, we applaud anyone who sincerely wants to become more like Christ. The Spiritual Formation Movement has recognized a genuine lack in the spiritual lives of many who claim to follow the Lord. Many have gone to church, read the Bible, spent time in prayer, and have a good handle on doctrine, but they have no quality of spiritual life. Admittedly, all of us experience dry spells in our spiritual journey and at such times we are vulnerable to a charismatic speaker, a well-written book, or a moving retreat. None of this is negative, unless what is being taught lacks biblical authority. At times these dry seasons are instruments of God to prepare our hearts for lessons He will teach. At other times we need to recognize that we may very well have left the path of true discipleship and need to return to the way laid out for us in the Word. The real danger is that we will turn to the wrong sources for our answers. This is what spiritual formation is doing.

Richard Foster wrote in 2004,

When I first began writing in the field in the late 70s and early 80s the term "Spiritual Formation" was hardly known, except for highly specialized references in relation to the Catholic orders. Today it is a rare person who has not heard the term. Seminary courses in Spiritual Formation proliferate like baby rabbits. Huge numbers are seeking to become certified as

Spiritual Directors to answer the cry of multiplied thousands for spiritual direction.[18]

This demonstrates well the popularity and spread of spiritual formation. Something that was only known in esoteric Roman Catholic circles less than 40 years ago is now demanding a front row seat in evangelical life. What has changed? The doctrines and teachings of Catholicism have not budged, but the willingness of evangelicals to compromise with the theology and practices of Rome have. As a matter of fact, even those who are soundly in conservative evangelical camps are willing to ignore huge doctrinal differences in order to experience a vitality of life that they, for whatever reason, have come to believe the Catholic contemplatives have to offer. Yet I believe that Michael Horton is correct when he warned,

> We want to have direct, intuitive supernatural experiences. But God has determined that we derive all our knowledge of Him, not through direct encounters, but through the written Word, the Bible, and in the Person and work of His incarnate Son.[19]

What Scripture offers in the way of Christian experience and what spiritual formation offers are two different things, as I hope to demonstrate in the chapters to come.

Conclusion

While some use "spiritual formation" as a synonym for discipleship, this is a mistake. However spiritual formation is officially defined, the means of spiritual formation within the movement is always spiritual disciplines drawn almost entirely from Roman Catholic and Eastern Orthodox mystics. Some evangelicals attempt to clean the disciplines up and redeem them for non-Catholic use, but the fact remains these disciplines are not taught in Scripture as channels for spiritual growth and discipleship.

Many are turning to spiritual formation at this time due to their own disappointments with their spiritual lives. When someone recommends the spiritual disciplines "which the church has always practiced throughout its history" (without mentioning that this is a reference to mystics within the Catholic and Orthodox traditions), some will naïvely jump at the opportunity. But as John MacArthur warns in another context,

> Lifeless, dry orthodoxy is the inevitable result of isolating objective truth from vibrant experience. But the answer to dead orthodoxy is not to build a theology on experience. Genuine experience must grow out of sound doctrine. We are not to base what we believe on what we have experienced. The reverse is true. Our experiences will grow out of what we believe.[20]

Spiritual dry spells and dead spots are an inevitable part

of the Christian life. Sometimes they are just normal mood cycles, at other times they are rooted in true spiritual concerns and sins. The disciple of Christ should pay attention to such times, for the Lord is at work. But the solution is not to turn to experiences and methods springing from the traditions of the past; it is found in returning to Scripture and through the power of the Holy Spirit living out the revelation the Lord has given us.

I must caution that the position I take will draw heavy criticism. Demarest attempts to ward off critiques of the Spiritual Formation Movement by saying, "The criticisms levied against the renewal of evangelical spirituality today reflects a lack of humility and charity. The excoriation of many Christian movements and leaders communicates the message that 'I alone have the truth' and 'the majority of faithful Christians today are wrong.'"[21] But this constitutes no argument at all, rather it is an attempt to silence and intimidate those who challenge spiritual formation. The proper rebuttal to Demarest is to argue that anyone claiming that "I alone have the truth" would be truly arrogant and lacking in charity. However, to claim that the Lord alone has the truth and He has revealed that portion of truth He wants us to know in Scripture (Deuteronomy 29:29) is a different matter. If in fact the Lord has given us the authoritative Word to teach us that which we should know and how we should live, it would seem the wisest, kindest and most God-honoring thing we could do is to believe, teach and live exactly as He has instructed us. In fact, it is the height of arrogance to do otherwise. Instead of chasing after the experiences and traditions of men we should rather delve deeply into the Word of God and live out the experiences He has designed for His followers.

2

Contemplative Prayer

Of all the spiritual disciplines the Spiritual Formation Movement promotes, none is more important than prayer and the intake of God's Word. On the surface we would expect little resistance to these two disciplines since they have been recognized as essential to spiritual growth by virtually all Christians from all traditions. Sadly, upon closer examination we discover that what is meant by most evangelical Christians when they reference prayer and Bible intake is not always what the leaders within spiritual formation mean. We begin with Donald Whitney, Associate Professor of Biblical Spirituality at Southern Seminary, who agrees with Carl Lundquist,

The New Testament church built two other disciplines upon prayer and Bible study, the Lord's Supper and small cell groups. John Wesley emphasized five works of piety by adding fasting. The medieval mystics wrote about nine disciplines clustered around three experiences: purgation of sin, enlightenment of the spirit and union with God. Later the Keswick Convention approach to practical holiness revolved around five different religious exercises. Today Richard Foster's book, *Celebration of Discipline,* lists twelve disciplines—all of them relevant to the contemporary Christian. But whatever varying religious exercises we may practice, without the two basic ones of Emmaus—prayer and Bible reading—the others are empty and powerless.[22]

In subsequent chapters I will shine the light of Scripture on many of these disciplines, but it is only proper and wise to begin with the two universally recognized as most important. As Whitney and Lundquist state, without prayer and Bible reading, all the other disciplines are empty and powerless. We begin with prayer, for its place in spiritual formation teachings is even more prominent than Bible study. Of course the position of prayer in the life of the believer is without question and needs little defense. Prayer is taught, modeled and expressed throughout the Bible. After the disciples had been with Jesus for a while and witnessed His life and power, they brought a request to Him: "Lord, teach us to pray." Jesus responded, not by giving them a rote prayer to repeat, but what we often call "The Lord's Prayer" as a model. The need and command to pray are seldom debated. Why we need to pray in the light of God's sovereignty and omniscience and how we pray are two different things. We pray, not because we have unraveled all the mysteries of prayer but because God tells us to pray and somehow, in the providence of God, our prayers really do matter.

How to pray gets more complex and is at the heart of the subject at hand. Scripture does not dictate a set amount of time to pray, nor does it approve or disapprove of particular postures in prayer. It does teach the need for both corporate and private prayers and it does model and instruct us on reasons to pray: to worship God, to bring our requests to Him, to thank Him, and to confess sin. What is important to notice throughout Scripture is that the individual who prays is speaking to God. While God communicates to us through the Bible, we respond to Him in prayer. The biblical paradigm of prayer is that of the believer approaching the Father in faith, through the mediatory ministry of Christ Jesus, in the power of the Holy Spirit, to communicate to God praise, thanksgiving, supplications and confession. While this pattern, which I will call throughout this book "biblical prayer," is never denied by those in spiritual formation circles, it is usually not what they have in mind when they speak of the discipline of prayer. Biblical prayer is our communication with God. As the Lord speaks to us through His Word, we speak to Him in prayer. Such prayers are rational, intelligent and flow from our minds. Paul said that he would pray with his spirit *and* with his mind also (1 Corinthians 14:15), not either/or. When we pray we are making use of our God-given intellect as we worship Him in spirit and truth (John 4:24). We are to pray without ceasing (1 Thessalonians 5:17) and in those prayers we are to make our requests known (Philippians 4:6). In prayer we praise God for His known attributes. In prayer we confess specific sins (1 John 1:9). Unfortunately biblical prayer, as described above, is not what spiritual formation advocates mean by contemplative prayer.

We need to take a hard look at contemplative prayer and ask some important questions: What is it and how does it differ from biblical prayer? How is it practiced? What is its goal? What is its origin? And why does it concern us?

What Is Contemplative Prayer?

First, as is common throughout the Spiritual Formation Movement, the catalyst offered for investigating the disciplines, including contemplative prayer, is the supposed insipidness of biblical praying. Larry Crabb, in his book *The PAPA Prayer*, frames it this way:

> [Biblical] praying to God is something like e-mailing a relative you've never met, who lives in a place you've never been. In return correspondence (to embellish the analogy), your relative never sends a picture of himself, never sends a picture of his house or land, and always writes a generic letter addressed to "My much loved relatives," like the ones we receive

every Christmas. His e-mails never come only to you and are therefore never addressed only to you. He never calls. And you can't call him. He has no phone.[23]

Crabb contrasts this impersonal type of prayer (as found in Scripture) with a contemplative form he calls the PAPA prayer making a promise to all who will use it, "I am promising Papa will speak to you. He loves a good conversation."[24] Who wouldn't be intrigued by such an offer?

So exactly what is contemplative prayer? It begins with detachment. Richard Foster, in his original 1978 edition of *Celebration of Discipline* wrote, "Christian meditation is an attempt to empty the mind in order to fill it" (p. 15). Fill it with what? In Eastern religions a person empties his mind in order to become one with the universe (or the Cosmic Mind). In Christian mysticism one empties the mind in order to become one with God. Foster quotes a number of mystics to describe this experience. For example there is Russian mystic Theophan the Recluse who said, "To pray is to descend with the mind into the heart, and there to stand before the face of the Lord, ever-present, all seeing, within you."[25] What Foster and Theophan mean by this is anyone's guess, but it is a vital part of the mystical experience.

Following detachment is the step of illumination, in which the newly emptied mind and heart is filled with supposed communication from God. The primary means of accomplishing illumination is through the use of the technique we are discussing: contemplative prayer. Contemplative prayer is the constant theme of the mystic, yet it is merely a means to an end which is union with God. The ultimate goal of the mystic, no matter what religion or tradition, is union with God (or gods, or in the case of pantheism, the universe) made possible through contemplative prayer. Mystics often claim to find union with God deep within their souls. Teresa of Ávila states, "As I could not make reflection with my understanding I contrived to picture Christ within me."[26] She is quoted as also saying, "Settle yourself in solitude and you will come upon Him in yourself."[27]

These types of experiences supposedly result not only in extrasensory contact with God but also communication from God. Richard Foster tells us, "We are to live in a perpetual, inward, listening silence so that God is the source of our words and actions."[28] Through these methods, especially that of contemplative prayer, a person is to empty his mind (detach) then fill it with imaginative experiences with Christ (attach) who he will find in the silence of his soul, resulting in God becoming the source of his words and actions. All of this unquestionably sounds attractive to many, even if no such teaching is found in Scripture.

The Goals
Digging a little deeper, there seems to be two overlapping

goals to contemplative prayer. The first is to encounter God in an inexplicable way. Ruth Haley Barton, well-known in spiritual formation circles and formerly on staff at Willow Creek Community Church, describes this desire,

> There are many terms that seek to capture this dynamic— silent prayer, centering prayer, contemplative prayer, interior prayer, prayer of the heart. Each carries a slightly different nuance, but they all are attempts to capture the same thing: the movement beyond words to an intimacy that requires no words. This intimacy is the kind that lovers know when they give themselves over to the act of lovemaking[29]

It should be noted that this type of erotic/romantic expression of the believer's relationship with God is historically common among the mystics.

Ruth Barton gives more details. She quotes Carlo Carretto, a Catholic mystic living just prior to the Reformation, "Thus the time comes when words are superfluous ... The soul converses with God with a single loving glance, although this may often be accompanied by dryness and suffering."[30] Barton describes contemplative prayer as a "deeper level of intimacy that will move us beyond *communication*, which primarily involves words and concepts, into *communion*, which is primarily beyond words. If there are any words at all, they are reduced to the simplest and most visceral expressions."[31] Later she writes, "You don't think your way into your breath prayer; you discover it by listening to your deepest longings and desires in God's presence."[32]

Those promoting contemplative prayer are not particularly interested in the mind. As a matter of fact, the mind gets in the way. It is the experience of somehow encountering God in an indescribable way that is desired. This is the goal of all true mysticism no matter what religion, and contemplation is the primary means used to accomplish this goal.

The second goal of contemplative prayer is to actually hear from God. John Ortberg, a former teaching pastor at Willow Creek Community Church and now senior pastor at Menlo Park Presbyterian Church, states, "It is one thing to speak to God. It is another thing to listen. When we listen to God, we receive guidance from the Holy Spirit."[33] While many evangelicals talk about the promptings of the Holy Spirit, Ortberg seems to be going further when he explains,

I certainly have no way to prove it was God speaking to me. A few friends have told me that early in life they were given a clear sense of what God was speaking to them. They learned to recognize certain movements of heart and mind as being the voice of God the way children learn to recognize the voice of their mother … I must be open to the possibility that sometimes God does speak directly to me … We must learn to listen for the still, small voice … In fact, being open and receptive to the leadings of the Holy Spirit is a non-optional part of transformation.[34]

Bruce Demarest writes, "Growing intimacy requires that I pay careful attention to the other person. When that other is God, it's necessary to still my own voice and listen in quietness. Then I can detect the gentle whispers of the Spirit. Too often we fail to hear God speak because we are not attentively listening."[35]

Richard Foster, the modern day authority most often consulted by contemplatives, wrote an entire book to convey this point. He opens *Sanctuary of the Soul* with these words, "Jesus Christ is alive and here to teach his people himself. His voice is not hard to hear; his vocabulary is not difficult to understand. But learning to listen well and to hear correctly is no small task."[36] He continues two pages later as he reviews his own experiences, "Now, I am not speaking here of an outward voice that can be captured by electronic equipment. That no doubt is possible, as the Bible gives ample witness. But here I am speaking of an inward whisper, a deep speaking into the heart, an interior knowing."[37] It is instructive to note that Foster does not seem to recognize that this "interior voice of God" has no biblical base. When he speaks of the audible voice of God, Foster can point to chapter and verse to at least indicate that God spoke audibly on occasion in biblical times.[38] But he cannot do so with inner voices from God, for in fact the Bible never mentions this type of interior message from the Lord. When God spoke in Scripture it was audible and objective, not internal and subjective. Foster, the contemplatives, and many others aligned with evangelicalism have invented a form of divine communication never found in Scripture. Even the "still small voice" borrowed from Elijah's experience (1 Kings 19:12–18) and used in almost all spiritual formation books was an actual voice, not an inaudible one heard only deep down in the interior of one's soul. Yet so important is it to hear God's voice in prayer that Foster quotes Elizabeth O'Connor saying, "This may be extremely difficult, for the churches have no courses on meditation, despite the fact that it is an art that must be learned from those who have mastered it, and despite the fact that the supreme task of the church is to listen to the Word of God."[39]

There are a number of things wrong with this statement. Foremost, the author is equating the supposed inner voices, which are being interpreted as from God, as the very "Word of God." This is important to note throughout spiritual formation literature. There are often disclaimers given by contemplatives to the effect that such revelations are not on par with the Scriptures, nor do these communications ever contradict Scripture. But the reality is that these perceived words are considered the very "Word of God" as O'Connor and Foster affirm. Tricia Rhodes writes, "Once I'm in that place of quiet, I often ask, 'Lord, what would you have me know right now? What would you have me consider?' Surprisingly enough, I often hear a specific word for that which lies in front of me."[40] Former evangelist Leighton Ford states, "It helps me to think[41] of 'abiding' as a continual conversation in which I listen for God's voice and speak back to him." Larry Crabb tells us that "Prayer is more about us hearing God than about Him hearing us. We're the audience."[42] This idea that we will hear directly from God, deep within the recesses of our souls, and therefore have a far more intimate relationship with Him, explains the draw of contemplative prayer. And while attractive, we have to ask: Where in Scripture is contemplative prayer taught? And where in Scripture are we told that prayer is about God talking to us rather than us talking to Him? And where in Scripture do we find any reference to God speaking to us within our spirits in an inaudible voice?

Another flaw in O'Connor's statement has to do with the idea that this form of listening to God must be taught by the spiritual masters ("those who have mastered it"). First, when the Lord spoke in Scripture, which was always audibly, no one had to teach the listener how to hear Him—they knew without taking lessons or reading books from anyone else that it was God speaking. Secondly the direct implication is that left to ourselves we will never be able to learn the art of hearing from God and if we don't become skilled at this art, we will be deficit in our spiritual development. Spiritual formation stands or falls on one's belief in extra-biblical, inner words from God that will be given only while practicing the art of contemplative prayer as taught by the "spiritual masters," i.e. Catholic and Orthodox mystics and their disciples.

Larry Crabb assures us, "I'm hearing from God in a way I haven't before. Sometimes, though never audibly, I hear the Father speak more clearly than I hear the voice of a human friend ... Let me tell you this: once you hear from God, you're hooked."[43] But Crabb and other contemplatives are not learning these doctrines and methods at the feet of Jesus as revealed in Scripture, but from the ancient Desert Fathers and Mothers and Catholic mystics both past and modern. The reason these techniques must be learned from the "spiritual masters" is because the inspired authors of God's Word said nothing about them, nor did Jesus. This certainly ought to say volumes to anyone truly wanting to know and do the will of God.

The Techniques

Speaking of techniques, just exactly how does one go about practicing contemplative prayer? Some of these have already been touched on above where the three-fold process of detaching, illumination and union are described. But let's take a closer look at the actual practices. When we do, we find that the techniques used and promoted by Christian contemplatives are virtually identical to those of Eastern religions, such as Buddhism, Hinduism and Jewish Kabala, and so are familiar to most of us through media presentations of transcendental meditation (TM) and yoga. Gary Thomas gives these rather common instructions to those wanting to practice contemplative prayer with the goal of encountering God in mystical fashion:

> Choose a word (Jesus or Father, for example) as a focus for contemplative prayer. Repeat the word silently in your mind for a set amount of time (say, twenty minutes) until your heart seems to be repeating the word by itself, just as naturally and involuntarily as breathing. But centering prayer is a contemplative act in which you don't do anything; you're simply resting in the presence of God.[44]

So, the repetition of words or short phrases, a mantra, is key to this experience. Barton agrees, but first she sets the mood: "Settle into a comfortable position that allows you to remain alert. Breathe deeply in this moment as a way of releasing any tension you might be holding and become aware of God's presence, which is closer than your breath. Allow yourself to enjoy God's presence in quietness for a few moments."[45] Mark Yaconelli, in his book *Downtime* which is designed to aid teens in developing the contemplative life, writes, "I sometimes invite students to a time of prayer by asking them to focus on the very simple act of breathing ... Close your eyes and simply notice your breathing ... Imagining with each in-breath that you are breathing in God's love, and with every out-breath you are releasing every distraction, every anxiety, every tension and resistance to God."[46]

Once you are in the right frame of mind you are ready for a mantra. Barton writes, "Choose your favorite name or image for God as you are relating to him right now, such as God, Jesus, Father, Creator, Spirit, Breath of life, Lord, Shepherd ..."[47]

What else? While Richard Foster suggests a number of methodologies, he says, "he finds it best to sit in a straight chair, with my back correctly positioned in the chair and both feet flat on the floor ... Place the hands on the knees, palms up in a gesture of receptivity. Sometimes it is good to close the eyes to remove distractions and center the attention on Christ. At other times it is helpful to ponder a picture of the Lord or to look out at some lovely trees and plants for the same purpose."[48] Brennan Manning gives these instructions in his book, *The Signature of Jesus*: "The first step in faith is to stop thinking about God in prayer ... Contemplative spirituality tends to emphasize the need for a change in consciousness ... we must come to see reality differently ... Choose a single, sacred word ... repeat the sacred word inwardly, slowly and often ... Enter into the great silence of God. Alone in that silence, the noise within will subside and the Voice of Love will be heard."[49]

Apparently the repetition of the mantra triggers the blank mind, or allows the mind and heart to detach. With the mind in neutral and the heart open to whatever voices or visions it encounters, accompanied with a vivid imagination, the individual enters into the mystical state. This is the state prized by mysticism and made possible through contemplative prayer. Concerning all of this Foster encourages, "Though it may sound strange to modern ears, we should without shame enroll as apprentices in the school of contemplative prayer."[50] By contrast, we search in vain to find any such encouragement or instruction in Scripture.

One of the most important aims of contemplative prayer, as we have already seen, is to hear the voice of Jesus, not audibly (at least not as a norm) but as "an inward whisper, a deep speaking into the heart, an interior knowing."[51] Foster assures us that many characters in the Bible had this experience, including Moses and Elijah.[52] What Foster and all promoters of mysticism fail to notice is that when biblical characters heard from God or angels they heard an audible voice, not an "inward whisper." For that reason, rarely does anyone in the biblical accounts ever question that he or she had heard from God. Not so the mystic who must "learn to hear the voice of God."[53] Foster assures us that in time we will be able to distinguish the voice of God from all others, including Satan's and our own. One way to determine this, we are told, is to remember, "Satan pushes and condemns, God draws and encourages. You can tell the difference."[54] Of course this is a gross over-generalization. We know, for example, that it is the Holy Spirit who convicts us of sin and judgment (John 16:8) and that God pronounces warnings and judgments throughout the Scriptures. Jesus Himself pronounced "woes" of judgment on the Pharisees who saw themselves as the spiritual leaders of Israel (Matthew 22:13–36); He clearly called Peter "Satan" at one point and told him to get behind Him, for Peter was a stumbling block to Him (Matthew 16:23). To characterize the Lord's voice as only one of drawing and encouragement would mean we would need to ignore huge portions of the Word of God.

In his book *Sanctuary of the Soul*, Foster offers three basic steps for contemplative prayer, which are a mere rephrasing of the threefold path of purgation, enlightenment and union. Foster calls his threefold pathway recollection, beholding and listening.[55] He defines these as follows:

- Recollection—letting go of all competing distractions, even good ones, until we have become truly present where we are. This can be done by focusing on a name, word or phrase.

- Beholding the Lord—"An inward steady gaze of the heart upon God, the divine Center … The soul, ushered into the Holy Place, is transfixed by what she sees."[56] During this phase some have experienced intense heat around their hearts;[57] others speak in tongues.[58]

- The prayer of listening—it is at this step that God speaks to us and we enjoy His full presence.[59]

The ultimate goal of these techniques is union with God, or what Foster calls, borrowing from the *Cloud of Unknowing*, "the contemplative life." Foster explains:

> The highest level, the contemplative life consists entirely in learning how to live in the presence of God. There is darkness here, but it is not a darkness of absence, but rather a darkness of incomplete knowing. We are carried into the "cloud" by love and sustained in it by gazing on God alone. We shut out every other source of stimulation—sensual, intellectual and reflective—in order to focus on God alone. At this level, we even move beyond our thoughts of God in order to dwell in his presence without thought or distraction. Of course, no one in this life can sustain this level of concentration for long ... But our calling is not to sidestep the opportunity but to recognize our own limits.[60]

This quote sums up both the methods and the aims of the contemplative life. Through various extra-biblical techniques, one enters into a sphere which is devoid of thought and feeling in an effort to experience the presence of God in an inexplicable manner. This is the union or ecstasy so prized by the mystic and found in all forms of mysticism. However it is not found or encouraged in Scripture. Contemplative life, as expressed by the spiritual formation leaders, put me in mind of something found in Isaiah in a different context. In Isaiah's day the people were turning not to God but to spiritists for hidden information. Isaiah tells them,

And when they say to you, "Consult the mediums and spiritists who whisper and mutter," should not a people consult their God? Should they consult the dead on behalf of the living? To the law and to the testimony! If they do not speak according to this word, it is because they have no dawn (Isaiah 8:19–20).

I am not accusing the contemplatives of being spiritists, but much like the spiritists they are seeking experiences and knowledge not sanctioned in Scripture. Thomas Merton wrote, "The life of contemplation ... is the life of the Holy Spirit in our inmost souls. The whole duty of contemplation is to abandon what is base and trivial in [your] own life, and do all [you] can to conform ... *to the secret and obscure promptings of the Spirit of God.*"[61] When Christians begin looking "to secret and obscure promptings," supposedly from the Holy Spirit, as taught by men and women of errant doctrine rather than Scripture, we are surely on shaky ground. We might do well to pay attention to the prophet Isaiah. Isaiah's warning to the Jews of his day is applicable to us now. He tells Judah, if people do not speak "according to this word, it is because they have no dawn." That is, the very ones who are claiming enlightenment and esoteric knowledge not found in Scripture don't know what they are talking about—so don't follow them. Instead turn to the law and to the testimony, i.e. the Word of God, for our source of truth.

Examples

Many evangelicals are turning to spiritual formation and the spiritual disciplines. Here is a sampling: Leighton Ford, former evangelist associated with Billy Graham, is now a strong adherent of spiritual formation. He describes his practice of contemplative prayer in this manner, "Often in the morning I will sit in a favorite chair in my study with a cup of coffee, with classical music playing, not trying to form a prayer with words but waiting, listening, until perhaps I sense the Spirit bringing to the surface a word from God. Then I offer just a simple 'Thank you.'"[62] Tricia McCary Rhodes draws on the fourth century Desert Fathers and Mothers to learn the art of "breath prayer" which is "to choose a phrase that is simple and heartfelt and can be offered to the Lord in one breath ... Once we've decided on the particular phrase, this then becomes the focus of our communion with Christ for a season. Some people like to repeat the prayer numerous times as they breathe in and out, quieting their heart before the Lord."[63] She tells us, "In this practice we take a few minutes to slow our breathing as we mentally inhale the reality of God's presence and exhale the noisy clamor inside us. We inhale the peace of Christ and exhale the anxiety of the day. We inhale cleansing for sin and exhale guilt and condemnation."[64]

On Rhodes' first attempt at breath prayer she "almost immediately ... heard the words, 'Give me a heart for you,' and I knew this was what I wanted and needed most—a renewal of yearning for the Lover of my soul."[65]

One of the most popular forms of contemplative prayer makes use of the "Jesus Prayer." Mike King, a pastor at Jacob's Well Church in Kansas City, writes in his book *Presence-centered Youth Ministry*,

> In the centuries after Jesus' resurrection, his followers sought ways to commune deeply with God. One form of prayer [was] respiratory prayer ... The most ancient prayer of this type is called the Jesus Prayer: "Lord Jesus Christ, Son of the Living God, have mercy on me, a sinner ..." With the inhale, pray the first part, "Lord Jesus Christ, Son of the living God." With the exhale, pray the second part, "Have mercy on me, a sinner."[66]

A more extensive example comes from the pen of Ruth Barton as she leads a leadership retreat,

> Recently our leadership community went on retreat to listen for God's direction ... Later on that day, one of the people who had heard about our decision [concerning a particular issue] sensed God saying, "You can help with that!" Having learned what the office space would cost, they sensed God's prompting to contribute the funds that would enable us to take the space for the year ... [In response Barton] sensed God saying very clearly, "You don't know what your future holds, but I do, and I know what you will need for that future. That is why I am

giving this to you." [She then heard God ask], "What do you do with gifts?" "You receive them," I heard myself answer. I heard God saying, "Stop your clinging and grasping, just receive what I am giving you and then build your ministry with that."[67]

Professor Bruce Demarest points his readers toward two post-Reformation mystics to illustrate the spiritual riches of the contemplative life.[68] The first is Counter-Reformation nun Teresa of Ávila whose "classic" book *Interior Castle* is a virtually incomprehensible description of mystical fantasy that spiritual formation disciples love. Having read the book, I seriously doubt that many have any idea what she is talking about as she describes her supposed visions from the Lord detailing seven rooms (or layers) of progressive experiences with God. Even more concerning is Demarest's second hero, Thomas Merton, a Trappist monk from Kentucky who died in 1968. No modern mystic besides Richard Foster has had more influence on the Spiritual Formation Movement than Thomas Merton. His work and promotion of contemplative prayer cannot be overestimated. Yet even Demarest admits that toward the end of Merton's life he became attracted to Eastern mysticism and believed that Zen meditation and Christian contemplation pursue the same goal. Ultimately he saw no difference between Buddhism and Christianity and once visited the Dalai Lama to "discover truth in dialogue."[69] Demarest disagrees with Merton at this point; nevertheless, he and most contemplatives look to Merton as a spiritual master and a guide to spiritual formation.

Conclusion

Spiritual formation seeks to lure evangelicals into ancient Catholic and Orthodox contemplative practices in order to draw closer to God, experience His presence, and hear His voice apart from Scripture. In order to embrace this mystical form of spirituality, contemplatives are willing to compromise at virtually every turn. Central doctrines such as *sola fide* and *sola Scriptura* are shrugged off as secondary. Methods never found in the Bible as the true means of spiritual growth and of knowing God, are emphasized. And complete heretics such as Thomas Merton are seen as reliable spiritual guides to spirituality. The contemplatives have sold out to Catholic mysticism and abandoned the clear teaching of Scripture. Sadly, in the process many undiscerning evangelicals will follow suit.

3

Sacred Reading (*Lectio Divina*)

As we have seen in the last two chapters, "Spiritual formation is an ancient ministry of the church, concerned with the 'forming' or 'shaping' of a believer's character and actions into the likeness of Christ."[70] Spiritual formation is distinguished from biblical discipleship primarily by its source of authority and its methodology. On the other hand discipleship as defined by the Bible turns to the Word of God as the final and ultimate authority over all matters of life and godliness. This means that if one truly desires to be a follower of Jesus Christ he will turn to the inspired Scriptures to determine both truth and how to "observe all that I [Christ] commanded you" (Matthew 28:20). Spiritual formation pays lip-service to Scripture but the true source behind the movement is the extrabiblical teachings and experiences of those in the past who supposedly have discovered the "secret" of deeper intimacy with God. Bruce Demarest says it this way: "For our help, [in the context of growth in the Spirit] we can turn to our Christian past—to men and women who understood how the soul finds satisfaction as we grow in God, and how His Spirit finds a more ready home in us."[71] Richard Foster and Gayle Beebe concur: "Through their reflections, the great saints witness to the work of the Holy Spirit and, when we study them, guide our spiritual life as well."[72] While Scripture is referenced by spiritual formation leaders, it is Scripture filtered through the experiences and insights of the "spiritual masters" as they are often called, that set the pace in spiritual formation.

From the above comments, and those of others with similar views, we clearly see that spiritual formation is different from the typical understanding of discipleship. Professor Demarest informs us that that difference lies not only in divergent authoritative sources but also in methodology and technique. He declares that some past saints have discovered "certain spiritual practices were highly effective in nurturing the inner man. These practices came to be known as the art and ministry of *spiritual formation*, a form of discipleship we are rediscovering today."[73] These practices are usually called "spiritual disciplines" and are the supposed means by which we become more like Christ. There are dozens of these disciplines, drawn almost entirely from Roman Catholic and Orthodox mystics and contemplatives throughout church history, which are being touted as essential to our spiritual life; however the two foundational ones are prayer and Scripture.

No evangelical would ever question the value of prayer and the Word in the process of sanctification but, as we are seeing, when the spiritual formation devotees speak of these disciplines they mean something entirely different from what Scripture does. Prayer to those promoting spiritual formation does not reference biblical prayer but contemplative prayer which was explained in the last chapter. Similarly, when spiritual formation enthusiasts promote the reading of the Bible they mean something very unlike the traditional reading, studying and applying of the Word of God to our lives. Foster agrees that "reading and studying and memorizing and meditating upon Scripture have always been the foundation of the Christian Disciplines. All of the Disciplines are built upon Scripture. Our practice of the Spiritual Disciplines is kept on course by our immersion in Scripture."[74] I have no argument with Foster's comment about the Word; it is what follows that is problematic. The breakdown comes in a seemingly innocent remark that completes Foster's quote, "So we must consider how we can

ourselves come to the Bible."[75] It is how we approach the
Bible, what we believe is its purpose, and how we understand
its interpretation that marks the distinction between biblical
discipleship's and spiritual formation's use of Scripture.

Briefly, conservative evangelicalism has taught that the
Bible is the inspired, infallible, inerrant and sufficient
Word of God whereby He reveals Himself, unfolds the
drama of redemption through Jesus Christ, draws man
to Himself and teaches him the truth necessary for godly
living now and eternal life to come. As 2 Timothy 3:16, 17
states, the Scriptures are "profitable for teaching, for reproof,
for correction, for training in righteousness; so that the
man of God may be adequate, equipped for every good
work." How the believer mines the treasures of Scripture
is through the normal, literal (often called grammatical/
historical) approach to its reading and study. As God's truth
is understood through this process it is then to be applied to
our lives through the power of the Holy Spirit. This is not the
approach to Scripture recommended and promoted within
spiritual formation. As a matter of fact this approach is often
ridiculed as merely an intellectual process that does not reach
the inner person and does not lead to transformation. Instead,
we are told that if our lives are to be truly changed by the
Bible we must turn to an ancient technique, never actually
taught in the Word itself, known as *lectio divina*.

Lectio Divina—a Definition

Lectio divina is a method of biblical meditation on the
Scriptures that has been practiced by some Christians
as far back as the fourth century. It is important to note
from the outset that no one knowledgeable of *lectio*, which
is sometimes called "sacred reading," "divine reading," or
"spiritual reading," claims that it is taught or modeled in
Scripture. Rather, it is a method created and first practiced by
contemplative Catholics three to four hundred years after the
time of Christ. Only recently, through the efforts of Richard
Foster and a host of others, has *lectio* gained a foothold
among Protestants, but its popularity is growing rapidly.
Foster believes *lectio* is rooted in the allegorical interpretation
of Scripture that reigned from the time of the early church
fathers such as Origen until the Reformation. Foster supposes
the pre-Reformation church saw an "interplay between God's
interpretive Spirit, our spirit and God's inspiring Spirit that
gave rise to the original text. Eventually, this method became
standardized and known as *lectio divina*, the oldest and most
widespread method for reading and understanding both the
literal and allegorical sense of Scripture."[76] This approach
to reading Scripture was one of the main issues at the time
of the Reformation, with the Reformers returning to the
original grammatical/historical method of understanding
the Bible. Foster believes the Protestant church was the loser
in this return to *sola scriptura* because *lectio* "originated with
the greatest minds in the history of the early and medieval
church. They were often sophisticated people with powerful

intellects."[77] Apparently the intellectual pedigree of the designers of *lectio* trumps the clear meaning of Scripture and how it was read through a normal, literal approach.

Lectio's modern attractiveness in the West stems from recent departures within the fields of philosophy and theology from literal, didactic thinking in tandem with a resurgence of imagination and experience based epistemologies. Foster even defines *lectio* as the means whereby "sanctified imagination" is used most frequently, in the reading of Scripture.[78]

In fact *lectio* has little to do with the knowledge of Scripture. Madame Guyon, well-known "Christian" mystic, writes, "[We are not to read the Scriptures to gain some understanding but to] turn your mind from outward things to the deep parts of your beings. You are not there to learn to read, but … to experience the presence of your Lord!"[79] Paraphrasing Guyon, Foster continues to claim, "It is not that we think about what we have read … it is that we feed on what we have read. Therefore we are to discipline our mind to be quiet before the Lord. We are to allow our mind to rest."[80]

Even Foster claims that Guyon's instructions are out of his range of experience, so we turn to Ruth Haley Barton, formerly on staff at Willow Creek Community Church, who writes, "*Lectio divina* is an approach to the Scriptures that sets us up to listen for the word of God spoken to us in the present moment … Invariably he communicates his love for us in ways that we can hear and experience *beyond cognitive knowing*. One of the reasons this approach is so powerful is that *lectio divina* involves a delicate balance of silence and word. It is a very concrete way of entering into the rhythm of speaking and listening involved in intimate communication."[81] *Lectio* is viewed as a means of hearing the voice of God in experiential, non-cognitive ways, so that in an inexplicable manner the Lord speaks to our hearts but not our minds. In *lectio* one does not go to the Scriptures to learn about God, or His ways, or to find and apply truth, but to experience a feeling of the presence of God. This is why Leighton Ford says that every morning as he "pray[s] the Scriptures" he "quietly sit[s] in the presence of my Lord, waiting for his voice."[82]

Lectio is used not only with Scripture but also when reading the saints of the past. The following quote by Richard Foster demonstrates how the contemplatives place on par with Scripture the writings of men and women.

We can learn from the lives of the saints and the writings that have proceeded from their profound experience of God. Humbly we read these writings because we know that God has spoken in the past ... So whether through Scripture, icons or the lives of faithful Christians down through the centuries, we are ever seeking to "descend with the mind into the heart, and there to stand before the face of the Lord."[83]

Mike King trains young people to meditate on Scripture to experience the Holy Spirit speaking to them. He recommends they keep a journal of their encounters with the Holy Spirit while practicing *lectio divina*. He instructs his students to listen "in quiet solitude for the Holy Spirit to speak to them individually." When their time of silence is complete they pair up to share what they sensed from the Holy Spirit.[84] Similarly at the 2013 Passion Conference, in Atlanta, Georgia, John Piper, Beth Moore, Francis Chan and Louie Giglio lead 45,000 college students through a modified guided *lectio divina* session. After the different speakers read a chapter from the book of Ephesians the participants were told to shut their eyes and listen to the voice of God. At the end of the experiment Giglio asked how many of the students (all under age 25) had heard the specific voice of God speaking to them. From the videos apparently the majority claimed they did.[85] Through such means, young adult Christians are being subtly introduced to spiritual disciplines such as *lectio divina*.

Kenneth Boa has written at least four books, all published by the Navigators's NavPress, teaching and promoting *lectio divina*: *Sacred Readings: A Journal*, *The Psalms: A Journal*, *The Trinity: A Journal*, and *Historic Creeds: A Journal*. Boa tells us:

Devotional spirituality revels in the glorious attributes of God and aspires to lay hold of God's aspiration for us. It prepares our souls for the "mystic sweet communion" of living entirely in God and in one another as the three persons of God eternally live and rejoice in one another. It instills in us a passion for Christ's indwelling life and inspires us to swim in the river of torrential love that flows from His throne of grace.[86]

Besides the fact that "mystic sweet communion" is not a biblical category but rather a phrase found in the hymn "The Church's One Foundation," and despite the fact that "living entirely in God and one another" is indeterminate in meaning, and despite the fact that being inspired "to swim in the river of torrential love that flows from His throne of grace" sounds inviting but is nebulous and nowhere found in Scripture, Boa believes that "devotional spirituality" should be the goal of every Christian. Strangely Boa does not see spiritual formation as resulting in deeper insights into God, but just the opposite. He writes,

> The great pilgrims [i.e. the ancient mystics] along the way have discovered that progress from superficial to substantive apprehension of God is not so much a movement from darkness to light as it is a pluming into the ever-increasing profundity of the cloud of unknowing.[87]

Lectio divina is, as Boa sees it, a formational reading as opposed to an informational reading of Scripture. By informational he means a linear approach that seeks to master (understand) the text through careful analytical

processes, as opposed to a formational approach which is
an in-depth process allowing the text to shape us without
much concern for its meaning. Boa says, "The formational
approach ... centers on speaking to the heart more than
informing the mind."[88] At best this division between heart
and mind is an artificial one. Biblically the heart references
the inner, immaterial part of mankind which includes the
mind. Besides, no place in Scripture are we ever told to
separate the heart from the mind or to attempt some form
of nonintellectual pursuit of God. Nevertheless, spiritual
formation in general, and *lectio divina* in particular, is
interested in experiences that cannot be explained or logically
understood; in a word: mystery.[89]

Boa explains that

Lectio divina centers on loving God through His Word.
It was introduced to the West by the Eastern desert father
John Cassian early in the fifth century. The sixth-century
Rule of St. Benedict that guided Benedictine and Cistercian
monastic practice prescribed daily periods for sacred reading.
Unfortunately, by the end of the Middle Ages it came to be
seen as a method that should be restricted to the spiritually
elite. As time passed, even monastics lost the simplicity of
sacred reading as it was replaced by more complicated systems
and forms of "mental prayer." In recent decades, however, this
ancient practice has been revitalized, especially by those in the
Cistercian tradition. Writers like Thomas Merton ... [and]

Thomas Keating ... have been promoting sacred reading in Catholic circles, and Protestants are now being exposed to this approach as well.[90]

In summary, *lectio* is a method for reading the Bible designed to feed the soul with minimum use of, or impact on, the mind. It was created by Catholic monks for those living in the monastic system and used almost exclusively within that monastic structure for centuries. It is never taught, alluded to or modeled by anyone in Scripture and lost favor even among Catholics at the latter stages of the Middle Ages. It was revitalized among some Catholics in the mid-1970s and more recently has increasingly caught the attention of Protestants. Eugene Peterson represents the attitude of many evangelicals in his endorsement of Richard Foster's *Celebration of Discipline*, which introduced spiritual formation, including *lectio*, to Protestants in the late 1970s,

Like a child exploring the attic of an old house on a rainy day, discovering a trunk full of treasure and then calling all his brothers and sisters to share the find, Richard Foster has "found" the spiritual disciplines that the modern world stored away and forgot, and has excitedly called us to celebrate them. For they are, as he shows us, the instruments of joy, the way into mature Christian spirituality and abundant life.[91]

With this description of *lectio divina*, along with the

background of its origin and use, we need next to move to methodology.

Lectio Divina—the Techniques

Sacred Reading proceeds in four stages: reading (*lectio*), meditation (*meditatio*), prayer (*oratio*), and contemplation (*contemplatio*). Sounds good on the surface, but as we dissect the stages we find that none of the stages is what evangelicals have traditionally understood when they speak of Bible reading and study.

Lectio: Richard Foster recommends a time of preparation before beginning to read. He writes, "Still yourself within by breathing deeply, quieting the clamor of demands and distractions. Do not rush this part. Inward stillness is as important to spiritual reading as muscle-stretching is to a workout."[92] After selecting a passage of Scripture, read it aloud, deliberately and slowly. "When you alight upon a word, a phrase, or a sentence that speaks to your heart pause in your reading."[93] It is important to note at this point that we are not reading the text looking for meaning, nor are we studying as "a 'scholar,' searching for information; instead come as a disciple who seeks insight from a learned mentor."[94] Mark Yaconelli explains the process,

Read a short passage two or three times, listening for a particular word that seems to stand out for us, address us, disturb us, or comfort us. We receive this word as if God were picking it up and handing it to us. We take this word and hold it within the deepest recesses of our heart. We repeat this word over and over, noticing the feelings and thoughts that come to us as we repeat this word gently within. We then allow ourselves to pray, to speak to God whatever words or feelings we have within us.[95]

Ruth Haley Barton adds that while reading we are to listen "for a word or phrase that strikes us … we have a sense of expectancy that God will speak to us. After reading there is a brief period of silence in which we remain with the word, savoring it and repeating it *without trying to figure out what it means or why it was given.*"[96]

Meditatio: the next step is meditation but not meditation as we normally would understand it. Boa describes meditation as "a spiritual work of holy desire and an interior invitation for the Spirit to pray and speak within us (Romans 8:26–27)."[97] Two brief thoughts before we move on. First, note the misinterpretation of Romans 8:26–27 which is virtually universal in mystical literature. The text does not promise that the Holy Spirit will speak to us in prayer but that He will intercede with the Father for us as we pray. This is an important and often overlooked point. Secondly, the emphasis throughout all four stages of *lectio* is on God speaking to us in the process. Foster writes,

Like the joyful awareness of a loved one whispering softly

into our ears, we become aware of the intimately personal voice of God. We cannot pinpoint where it is coming from because suddenly it is *within* us, sounding with a heightened clarity and immediacy, reverberating in the chambers of our heart. We know without a doubt who is speaking to us. Jesus is the Good Shepherd, and his sheep know his voice.[98]

Rather than turning us to the Word of God to hear the Lord's voice, *lectio* turns us inward to attempt to listen to a subjective thought that is being interpreted as from the Lord. In addition, Barton cautions her readers not to think too much about the passage at this stage, rather "keep coming back to the word that we have been given."[99] The word "given" to one of the students of Yaconelli, while reading about Jesus sitting in a boat, was "cushion." The young man repeated the word "cushion" over and over "for the longest time" until he started to remember his grandmother lying on a pillow just before she died, the youth felt so peaceful he nearly went to sleep.[100] This was supposedly the message that God was speaking to this teenager from Mark 4:35–41. This is hardly deep spiritual insight.

Oratio: Most evangelicals understand reading of the Word as God speaking to us; in turn we speak to Him through prayer. But *oratio* is more complicated than that: "*Oratio* is a time for participation in the interpenetrating subjectivity of the Trinity through prolonged mutual presence and growing identification with the life of Christ."[101] If this statement by Ken Boa leaves you scratching your head join the club. Richard Foster uses the language of mystical romanticism to describe the same thing,

> We want to turn to the Lover who is whispering in our ear and look in the divine face, trace with our fingertips the beloved features while speaking softly in return, and rejoice to see ourselves reflected in Jesus' gaze and feel our very existence affirmed by his intimate awareness of us.[102]

In *oratio* the participant is listening for the voice of God as much as actually praying to the Lord. But more importantly, prayer in *lectio divina* is "part of the path that leads to contemplation"[103]—the actual goal of *lectio*.

Contemplatio: Tricia McCary Rhodes writes,

> The final step in *lectio divina* is *contemplation*, which means to focus on being aware of God's presence, drawing near and loving him. If we speak at all during this time, it is to offer words of gratitude for what we've seen or to express the love we feel in our hearts toward the Lord. Often we will sit quietly, even if only for a moment or two, musing over the wonder that the God of the universe has broken into our day with a personal revelation.[104]

This is the Holy Grail in *lectio divina* in which the Lord provides a personal revelation to those who have taken the four steps. Boa describes this fourth step as "a mysterious territory in which the language is silence and the action is receptivity. True contemplation is a theological grace that cannot be reduced to logical, psychological, or aesthetic categories."[105] This same author clearly distinguishes meditation and contemplation. Meditative prayer involves speech, activity, discursive thought, vocal and mental prayer, natural faculties of reason and imagination, affective feelings, reading and reflection, doing, seeking, and talking to Jesus. Contemplative prayer is described as silence, receptivity, loss of mental images and concepts, wordless prayer and interior stillness, mysterious darkening of the natural faculties, loss of feelings, inability to meditate, being receiving, and entering into the prayer of Jesus.[106]

As can be seen, contemplation within the spiritual formation movement is entering into a mysterious, virtual trance-like state in which one believes he has achieved union with God. Boa frames it this way: "When we enter into the numinous territory of contemplation, it is best for us to stop talking and 'listen to Him' in simple and loving attentiveness. In this strange and holy land we must remove the sandals of our ideas, constructs, and inclinations, and quietly listen for the voice of God."[107] Modern mystic Thomas Merton adds, "The life of contemplation … is the life of the Holy Spirit in our inmost souls. The whole duty of contemplation is to abandon what is base and trivial in (your) own life, and do all (you) can to conform ... *to the secret and obscure promptings of the Spirit of God.*"[108]

It should also be noted that the contemplatives believe *lectio divina* should be used with other literature outside of the Bible. God will speak to us in the creeds, Boa believes. Demarest tells us that "God also graciously speaks to His children through Christian books, hymns and religious art."[109]

Conclusion

Lectio divina is the counterpart to contemplative prayer within spiritual formation. As contemplative prayer is a mystical, non-cognitive method of prayer which has as its goal an inexplicable union with God, so *lectio* uses the same approach with the same goal in regard to Scripture. The motivation behind this system is the oft' expressed concern that Christian living in the West has been reduced to mere mental activity. Morton Kelsey observes that "In Protestantism, God became a theological idea known by inference rather than a reality known by experience."[110]

In analyzing this concern it is important to understand that it is largely a straw man. There are exceptions to be sure, but I know of no one who desires or teaches that the Christian life should be only cerebral, or simply a theological knowledge of a set of facts. Rather, biblical Christianity teaches that our lives are to be shaped by truth—truth that

forms us into Christ-likeness. Without the application
of truth, through the power of the Holy Spirit, we will
become spiritually stunted, but that is neither the thrust of
Scripture nor the teaching of the vast majority of evangelical
leaders and churches. The distinction between contemplative
spirituality and conservative evangelicalism lies first of all in
the dominate or controlling factor. For the spiritual formation
movement the ruling element is experience and imagination.
For the evangelical it is truth emanating from the Scriptures.

This leads naturally into the source of truth. Conservative
Christians believe that the final authority for life, doctrine
and experience is the Word of God (2 Timothy 3:16–17).
If the Bible teaches something then we trust it, put it into
practice, and live it. But if a claim or teaching aimed toward
spiritual life and development is not found in the Scriptures,
it is at best an opinion and certainly not a dogma to be cloned
and distributed among God's people. Spiritual formation
leaders, however, do not find their teachings and practices
in Scripture but in the writings of ancient mystics that have
been revitalized by modern admirers. This is what separates
biblical Christianity from spiritual formation and should
be able to convince any tempted by spiritual formation to
reexamine carefully the claims, experiences, and methodology
of the movement.

4

Solitude and Silence

In a world filled with noise, many of us long to "unplug" and find a quiet spot far from the hum of technology, the demands of work, the cries of children, the ubiquitous call of advertisement, the hype of politicians and the bombardment of world news. To escape, even for a few minutes, and find rest for our souls is an almost universal longing in modern times, especially in the West. When this rest is accompanied with time alone with God, it provides the refreshment and strength that we need to face the pressures of everyday living in a fast-paced age. For these reasons, when spiritual leaders start talking about silence and solitude, our ears perk up and we yearn to adopt the teachings and techniques they recommend. For most of my lifetime I have heard people refer to their habit of regular prayer and Bible study as a "quiet time." And while the term "quiet time" does not completely describe this valuable occasion alone with God, it does depict one aspect of it—a time set apart to quietly meditate on the Word and pour our hearts out to God. All this to say that I treasure quiet and solitude as much or more than most Christians. I constantly recommend it to the church I pastor. I would not be able to function spiritually without time alone daily with the Lord and I suspect the same is true for all of us.

But when the leaders of the Spiritual Formation Movement speak of quiet and solitude they are referencing something very different from a "quiet time" comprised of Bible reading and prayer. In the previous two chapters, I have documented how the spiritual formation leaders redefine prayer and Bible study and they have done the same with silence and solitude. We need to keep in mind that spiritual formation is the movement which makes certain disciplines absolutely essential for spiritual development. The problem lies in the fact that these disciplines, as they are being defined, are not drawn from Scripture but mostly from ancient Catholic mystics, monks, hermit and nuns. As a result, even as spiritual formation leaders use some of the same terms found in Scripture, they are actually calling for activities that are not rooted in the Word. We have already seen in previous chapters that the two principle disciplines recommended within spiritual formation are prayer and Bible reading, and who would argue with that? But biblical praying has been twisted into "contemplative" prayer which is an attempt to experience mystical union with God through certain methods never found in Scripture. The same is true of Bible reading which is turned into *lectio divina* (sacred reading), a mystical form of approaching the Bible that is very similar in technique and aim as contemplative prayer and again is missing on the pages of the Bible. Within spiritual formation, contemplative prayer, and *lectio divina* are foundational. Everything else in its teachings rests on these two disciplines. But flowing from these is a host of other lesser disciplines which vary from writer to writer. I want to focus the remaining chapters in this first section of the book on these lesser disciplines beginning with silence and solitude which is recommended by all contemplative authors and leaders. As we will see, when spiritual formation speaks of these two disciplines, they do not mean what most of us would expect and they do not base much of what they teach on the Word of God.

Silence and Solitude in Scripture

Before we delve more deeply into the spiritual formation teachings on silence and solitude, we should first confirm that the Bible does in fact teach the value of both. We find that Jesus was led by the Spirit into the wilderness for forty days of testing (Luke 4:1ff) and that He was in the habit of going alone to pray (Matthew 14:23; Mark 1:35; Luke 4:42).

The Lord apparently taught Paul in the Arabian desert for three years before He launched him into ministry (Galatians 1:17–18). It was on the Island of Patmos that John received the Revelation (Revelation 1:9–10). Virtually every one of the major Old Testament prophets, right through the time of John the Baptist, were men of solitude. It would appear that the Lord does some of His best work in our lives when we are separated from the crowd and in a place where we can quietly reflect on Him. At the same time, as Bruce Demarest remarks, there are no entries under "quietness," "silence," or "solitude" in the popular *Nave's Topical Bible*.[111] Also there exists no command in Scripture to seek solitude in order to be spiritually transformed. The individuals mentioned above were either taken into solitude by the Lord or chose for whatever reason to seek solitude. But a pattern we discern in a biblical character does not demand a practice on our part, unless the Scriptures specifically tell us to do the same. An example may provide some helpful instruction and insight but it does not constitute a mandate.

Spiritual formation teachers often attempt to establish a biblical requirement for solitude/silence by turning to passages they either take out of context or clearly misinterpret. Psalm 46:10 is a favorite which in the KJV is translated, "Be still and know that I am God." However, the immediate context has nothing to do with solitude or silence but instead carries the idea that we should cease striving in our attempts to overcome our enemies and recognize the

Lord's sovereignty over all things. This is why the opening words are translated "cease striving" in the NASB, "be still" in ESV and "stop your fighting" in HCSB. Demarest attempts to proof-text the mandate for solitude/silence with an out-of-context quote from Isaiah 30:15 which is a warning to Old Testament Judah not to rely on Egypt for aid. He also misinterprets Habakkuk 2:20 and Zechariah 2:13, both of which call on us to trust God but have nothing to do with the disciplines of silence/solitude. And he seriously misapplies 1 Peter 3:4 which calls for wives to be known by their gentle and quiet spirits, not be silent for the purpose of spiritual formation.

Of course every adherent of contemplative spirituality's favorite passage on this subject is Elijah's "still small voice" (1 Kings 19:12–13). For example, Ruth Haley Barton tells us, "Elijah's willingness to enter into solitude and silence opened room for God to minister to him in ways he had not yet experienced"[112] (p. 19). Even a cursory reading of the account finds that Elijah had no desire to enter into solitude and silence as Barton describes it. He was running for his life from Jezebel, depressed and ready to entirely give up his life as a prophet. God graciously reached out and restored His man, but Elijah wasn't looking for an experience with God. Additionally there is no command anywhere in Scripture to try to duplicate Elijah's example. Simply put, while seeking a quiet place to be alone with God is without question a good idea and is exemplified in Scripture, it is not commanded and is never taught as essential for discipleship.

The Goal of Silence/Solitude

It is important to understand that in using the discipline of silence/solitude, spiritual formation leaders are looking for something beyond discipleship; they are looking for a personal word, a message, a revelation, from the Lord. This is why Elijah's experience is so prominent in all contemplative writings. The idea is, if Elijah went alone and heard the "still small voice of God," then if we follow in his footsteps we will experience the same.

The attraction of silence/solitude within contemplative circles is the belief that in silence God will show up and speak to us independent from the Scriptures. M. Basil Pennington says it like this,

God is infinitely patient. He will not push himself into our lives. He knows the greatest thing he has given us is our freedom. If we want habitually, even exclusively, to operate from the level of our own reason, he will respectfully keep silent. We can fill ourselves with our own thoughts, ideas, images, and feelings. He will not interfere. But if we invite him with attention, opening the inner spaces, with silence, he will speak to our souls, not in words or concepts, but in the mysterious way that Love expresses itself—by presence.[113]

This goal of hearing the voice of God through use of these disciplines will be documented below. For now let's take a closer look at solitude.

Solitude

While many attempt to distinguish between the two disciplines Richard Foster, in his groundbreaking book *Celebration of Discipline*, does not believe this is possible: "Without silence there is no solitude," he informs us.[114] And while he is no doubt correct, I will attempt to distinguish between the two for the purpose of our analysis. Donald Whitney, who does not advocate contemplative spiritual disciplines, as defined by Foster and Willard, defines "the discipline of silence [as] the voluntary and temporary abstention from speaking so that certain spiritual goals might be sought," while "solitude is the Spiritual Discipline of voluntarily and temporarily withdrawing to privacy for spiritual purposes."[115]

Dallas Willard elevates the value of solitude when he states, "Solitude frees us, actually. This above all explains its primacy and priority among the disciplines ... Nothing but solitude can allow the development of a freedom from the ingrained behaviors that hinder our integration into God's order."[116] In the forward to Ruth Haley Barton's book *Invitation to Solitude and Silence*, Willard adds,

Solitude and silence are the most radical of the spiritual

disciplines because they most directly attack the sources of human misery and wrongdoing. To be in solitude is to choose to do nothing. For extensive periods of time. All accomplishment is given up. Silence is required to complete solitude, for until we enter quietness, the world still lays hold of us.[117]

If solitude is such a powerful discipline what exactly is the goal behind it? For one thing, the mystics believe the power of transformation is found in solitude. Roman Catholic contemplative Henri Nouwen wrote, "Solitude is the furnace of transformation."[118] Just how does solitude produce transformation? This is far more complicated than one might expect. We need to back up and recall that the ultimate goal of all mysticism is an unmediated encounter with the divine being (e.g. God in the case of Christianity, the universe in the case of Buddhism, the spirit world in the case of animism, Allah in the case of Islam). With this in mind, Barton informs us that "the longing for solitude is the longing for God. It is the longing to experience union with God unmediated by the ways we typically try to relate to God. By 'unmediated' I mean a direct experience of God with nothing in between, an encounter with God that is not mediated by words, by theological constructs …"[119] Solitude, as spiritual formation leaders understand it, is a tool that aids in bringing about union between our souls and God. What complicates the process is that our souls are not fond of such encounters. Parker Palmer tells us,

The soul is like a wild animal—tough, resilient, resourceful, savvy, self-sufficient. It knows how to survive in hard places. But it is also shy. Just like a wild animal, it seeks safety in the dense underbrush. If we want to see a wild animal, we know that the last thing we should do is go crashing through the woods yelling for it to come out. But if we will walk quietly into the woods, sit patiently by the base of the tree, and fade into our surroundings, the wild animal we seek might put in an appearance.[120]

How Palmer is so knowledgeable of the behavior of the soul is a bit of a mystery, given that nothing like this is even remotely taught in Scripture. Nevertheless, the idea is that if we want to get our shy little soul to cautiously come out to play, we will need to coax it with solitude. Barton equates the soul with ourselves and writes, "The longing for solitude is also the longing to find ourselves ... This is our soul, that place at the very center of our being that is known by God, that is grounded in God and is one with God. But it's tricky to get the soul to come out."[121] It is through solitude that an encounter with God is brokered for, as Teresa of Ávila promises, "Settle yourself in solitude and you will come upon Him in yourself."[122]

One of the ultimate experiences of mysticism, and a direct goal of solitude, is to stumble upon the "dark night of the soul." The dark night of the soul originated with a Counter-Reformation monk known as St. John of the Cross. His book, by the same title, is considered one of the most important and influential texts within contemplative circles. Richard Foster promises that to take seriously the discipline of solitude will mean that at some point or points along the pilgrimage we will enter 'the dark night of the soul.'"[123] The dark night is not a period of depression; it is "a divine appointment, a privileged opportunity to draw close to the divine Center."[124] What is involved in this dark night?

> We may have a sense of dryness, aloneness, even lostness. Any overdependency on the emotional life is stripped away … When solitude is seriously pursued, there is usually a flush of initial success and then an inevitable letdown—and with it a desire to abandon the pursuit altogether. Feelings leave and there is the sense that we are not getting through to God … the darkness of the soul … put the sensory and spiritual appetites to sleep … it binds the imagination and impedes it from doing any good discursive work. It makes the memory cease, the intellect become dark and unable to understand anything, and hence it causes the will also to become arid and constrained, and all the faculties empty and useless. And over all this hangs a dense and burdensome cloud which afflicts the soul and keeps it withdrawn from God.[125]

This rather numb, mindless, emotionless, trance-like state is supposedly necessary in order for the Lord to transform us. St. John of the Cross tells us that "by walking in darkness the soul … advances rapidly, because it thus gains the virtues." [126]

And yet all of this is drawn from a sixteenth century monk and not from the inspired Word of God. It is worth asking at this point, why should the child of God seek an experience that is neither authorized nor patterned in the Scriptures but was invented by a man who spent much of his life attempting to win back to the Catholic Church those who had left during the Reformation? Examining the root of most systems of thought ultimately will explain the fruit.

Silence

Even writers who differ a great deal about what the Bible teaches in these matters—such as Foster and Whitney quoted above—affirm that silence and solitude work in tandem. Solitude without silence is ineffective and silence without solitude is anemic. Dallas Willard tells us, "Silence and solitude do go hand in hand, usually. Just as silence is vital to make solitude real, so is solitude needed to make the discipline of silence complete. Very few of us can be silent in the presence of others."[127] However, silence seems to trump solitude for Willard writes, "Silence goes beyond solitude, and without it solitude has little effect. Henri Nouwen observes that 'silence is the way to make solitude a reality.'"[128]

The two disciplines, however, supposedly work together for the same purpose—encountering God and hearing His voice apart from Scripture. Willard says, "Only silence will allow us life-transforming concentration upon God. It allows us to hear the gentle God whose only Son 'shall not strive, nor cry;

neither shall any man hear his voice above the street noise'
(Matthew 12:19)." As is common, Willard is ripping a verse
out of context to attempt to prove his point. Matthew 12:19 is
about the incarnation and ministry of Jesus during His time
on earth and has absolutely nothing to do with the discipline
of silence. Willard uses the verse however to try to press upon
his readers the need to become silent enough to be able to
hear the apparently quiet voice of Jesus. John of the Cross (d.
1591) agrees, "The Father utters one Word. That Word is his
Son, and he utters Him forever in the everlasting silence. In
silence the soul has to hear him."[129]

This may sound strange, even incomprehensible, and it
is but, according to Mark Yaconelli, "Silence is God's first
language"[130] and, "Silence leads to prayer. Prayer leads to faith.
Faith leads to service. Service leads to peace."[131] But more
than this, "Silence is how we learn to listen and discern the
voice of God."[132] The value, importance and draw of silence
in contemplative circles is this promise that God will speak
to us out of the silence. Richard Foster writes, "In the quiet
of those brief hours, listen to the thunder of God's silence."[133]
I am not sure what the "thunder of God's silence" could even
be, but apparently it is at such times that God supposedly
speaks to us in this manner.

Most involved in any form of mysticism are quick to
downplay these revelations from God by saying they are
not on par with Scripture. Yet, while I will agree that not

every revelation that God has given, even in biblical times, was recorded in Scripture, I reject any notion that any form of revelation from God is inferior to another. When the Lord speaks it is with absolute authority; it is inerrant, it is infallible, it is to be obeyed. So-called fresh words from the Lord today, communication not found in the Bible, if they were authentic would be every bit as inspired as Scripture. The Lord does not have two forms of communication—one that is totally His Word, coming with complete authority, and one that is somewhat less than His Word and lacking authority. Regardless, Foster tells us to "keep a journal record of what comes to you."[134] This seems suspiciously similar to authoritative Scripture to me. We are now told to journal what God is saying to us, apparently for future reference. So is God speaking to people who practice the discipline of silence? If so, is this revelation inspired (is there any other kind of revelation from God?). And if we are now writing down these inspired revelations and keeping them in a journal, in what sense are they not Scripture, at least to the one believing they are hearing from God? This whole concept is a slippery slope.

Barton tells of times when God has spoken to her specifically, but this begs the question, and she realizes it, of how one knows the voice of God when she hears it. The author never really answers this question, retreating first to assumptions: "One of the basic assumptions of the Christian life is that God does communicate with us through the Holy

Spirit."[135] Why she assumes that the Holy Spirit speaks to the Christian directly is not explained, especially since the inner voice of God that she is championing is never once found in any scriptural account. Yet Barton promises us "through practice and experience we become familiar with the tone of God's voice [and] we learn to recognize God's voice."[136] Since this really doesn't answer the question, she assures us that learning God's voice will "take experience and practice."[137] Therefore, in order to support an unwarranted and biblically indefensible idea that God speaks to us apart from Scripture, and often without words in our inner being,[138] the best that Barton can offer is that eventually we will be able to distinguish God's voice from our own if we just keep practicing. This is disappointing at best. But to make things worse, apparently God "is speaking to us all the time" and we are obligated to obey what He says.[139] This puts an unsustainable burden on those who accept Barton's ideas as they must not only hear the inner, wordless voice of God, they must also obey it. If they do not they would of course be in sin.

Techniques

If a person desired to practice the discipline of silence how should they go about it? Demarest offers the following exercises for "stilling the soul": listening to classical music, taking a quiet walk in nature, and other more disciplined regimens such as focusing on our breathing.[140] More specifically he recommends to "sit comfortably, and just breathe normally. As you breathe, focus attention on the air as it enters and leaves your nostrils. Should your mind wander, gently bring the focus back to awareness of your breath. Continue this for several minutes … Its benefits are heightened emotional composures and, more importantly, greater receptiveness to God."[141] Demarest also recommends another similar quieting exercise:

Again breathe normally. As you exhale, imagine with God's help that you are breathing spiritual and emotional impurities out of your life. These might include worry (see Luke 12:22, 25–26), fear (see 1 John 4:18), or anger (see Psalm 37:8; Colossians 3:8). Focus for a few moments on one impurity, then on another. This act of the will aids conscious release of sinful impulses—a silencing of the false-self that Scripture describes as the "old man" (KJV) or the evil nature (see Romans 6:6; Ephesians 4:22, Colossians 3:9). Focus on your inhalations. Imagine, with God's help, that you are breathing in positive graces commended by Scripture … This act of the will amounts to a conscious appropriation of biblical virtues—an enhancing of the true self that Scripture calls the "new man" (KJV) or the "new nature" (see Ephesians 4:24; Colossians 3:10). Physically and emotionally, these exercises promote realization. Spiritually, they facilitate dismissal of the sinful self and enhancement of the new nature in Christ. Such exercises acknowledge our created humanity—that God made us as souls in physical bodies.[142]

We can glean from this lengthy quote, as well as the previous ones from Professor Demarest, two important things. First, the techniques recommended are not drawn from Scripture; at best they are optional. If listening to classical music or talking a walk in nature is comforting and helpful to you there would be no reason not to do these things. However, the Lord never mentions such exercises as needed to prepare our hearts for spiritual formation. The breathing exercises have much closer ties to Eastern mysticism than anything found in biblical Christianity. Secondly, and more importantly, these breathing exercises are not prescribed in Scripture as a means of putting off the old man or putting on the new man. They do not, as promised, "facilitate dismissal of the sinful self and enhancement of the new nature in Christ." The promises given are simply false. If it calms you to concentrate on your breathing there is nothing in Scripture that prohibits you from doing so. However, the spiritual claims being touted cannot be substantiated by the Word. These ideas were invented by mystics centuries ago and are now being passed on by their disciples. But neither Jesus nor any of the apostles practiced these methods nor, more importantly, taught others to do the same.

Barton also adds the use of a mantra (although she never calls it such) in our time of silence in order to facilitate hearing the voice of God.[143] She tells her readers to "ask for a simple prayer (from God)," such as "Here I am," or "Come, Lord Jesus." She writes, "It is best if the prayer is no more than six or eight syllables so that it can be prayed very naturally in the rhythm of your breathing ... Pray this prayer several times as an entry into silence and also as a way of dealing with distractions."[144] Mantras play an important role in all forms of mysticism and they do so here as well, but are never taught in the Word of God.

Monasticism

A word about monasticism is appropriate in this context, since most of the spiritual disciplines and especially solitude/silence were invented and perfected by the hermits and monks in ancient Christianity. The roots of monasticism were formed when Christianity became the state religion and persecution ceased. Until the time of Constantine, believers often battled persecution and martyrdom. In such an environment the differences between the church and the world were quite clear. But when Christianity was legalized and adopted as the official state religion in AD 311, impurity entered the church quickly. Some longed to separate themselves from this corruption and chose to do so by becoming hermits—many of whom were later called "desert fathers" since they moved into the Egyptian desert for refuge in an attempt to pursue holiness. The best known of these hermits was Antony whose life was chronicled by Athanasius (d. 396). However, living alone under such circumstances was quite dangerous and soon these hermits created communities in which they could practice solitude in safety (even though it is quite ironic to think of a community of hermits). These communities were enclosed by protective walls for safety but each hermit had his separate dwelling in order to live in solitude. From this arrangement, what we know as monasteries eventually emerged.

In recent times, as the spiritual disciplines and spiritual formation become more popular, so has monasticism. The term "new monasticism" is becoming common on the Internet and among emergent and mystical-oriented writers such as Richard Foster, Tony Jones and Brian McLaren. The Winter 2007 issue of *Christian History and Biography* is devoted to the monasticism of sixth-century monk St. Benedict and states, "No topic touches young evangelical students more than monasticism."[145] Why would this be true? Perhaps because the fragmented, success oriented, materialistic age is running out of gas for many. Something more appears to be needed, something with depth, something beyond the superficial entertainment-oriented Christian tradition to which many have grown accustomed, and has become a normal way of life. Between the combination of restlessness/disillusionment and the promise of better things in solitude, asceticism and a life of spiritual discipline, monasticism has a certain draw. To be sure, this is a "new monasticism" with a 21st century twist. The origin of early Christian monasticism came in the fourth century following the legalization of Christianity. Until then martyrdom was

the ultimate test of devotion, [but at that point] ... the Christian ascetic inherited the mantle of the martyr ...

[becoming sort of a living martyr] ... Monks sought to live an angelic life on earth, neither marrying nor having children. By refusing to participate in the continual process of physically repopulating the earth, they recognized that Christ's coming had initiated a new age and believed that their lives could help usher in his kingdom.[146]

Contemporary young people attracted to monasticism are not likely to abandon conventional life and live as hermits in caves or even monasteries. More commonly they will continue to keep their jobs, live in standard dwellings with family or friends and carry out the normal activities of modern society. But they, as do so many of us, are yearning for some sense of serenity, quieter and simpler times, and therein lays the pull of monastic and ancient practices. Desire can be a harsh taskmaster whenever it is not focused on truly biblical pursuits.

As more evangelicals become familiar with the disciplines that are drawn from the monks and nuns who originated these exercises, there has been a growing interest among a number to have a similar experience. Some, such as Larry Crabb and Leighton Ford, are going to monasteries for a week or more to spend time in silence and solitude. Others, such as Bruce Demarest, have participated in spiritual retreats at monasteries led by Catholic monks, to learn more about this way of life. It is from exposure to these influences, not new findings in Scripture, which has brought these Protestant evangelicals into the Spiritual Formation Movement. Brian McLaren is right (I don't say that often) when he acknowledges, "Many Christian leaders started searching for a new approach under the banner of 'spiritual formation.' This new search has led many of them back to Catholic contemplative practices and medieval monastic disciplines."[147] This statement constitutes a good warning to those who think they can imbibe in the contemplative spiritual disciplines and not be taken in by the theology behind them.

5

Spiritual Formation
at Worship

Within spiritual formation and similar circles, there has been much criticism of worship as found in evangelical Protestantism. Much of this criticism is aimed at the seeker-sensitive churches with their push for polished performances, entertainment, and the desire to keep the seeker (i.e. unsaved people who are attending the services) as comfortable as possible by offering them an environment and experience similar to what they would encounter at a secular gathering or concert. The idea is that people unfamiliar with church life feel more at home and will be more likely to return if they do not encounter something foreign or "weird" in the form of worship. This approach is obviously working, if one evaluates a church on the basis of nickels and noses, as the largest churches in the world have adopted this philosophy. But there has been a considerable push back against this viewpoint within not only more conservative evangelical churches but also from the emergent and spiritual formation camps. Mike King believes the church should offer an alternative experience and states, "It should be a bit odd and peculiar for visitors to enter our sanctuaries and engage in worship. This isn't bad. It's good. It shows that we are a subculture that's distinct."[148] And Dan Kimball observes that "many of these very things [methods promoted by the seeker-sensitive movement] are contrary to what emerging generations value and are seeking in their spiritual experience … The things that seeker-sensitive churches removed from their churches are the very things nonbelievers want to experience if they attend a worship service. So I don't think there will be much controversy about bringing back all the spiritual elements and going deeper with our teaching!"[149]

It would be hoped that many who have grown tired of the splash and show of consumer-oriented, market-driven strategy would seek out biblically-based churches that major on Christ, the gospel and Scripture. There are many churches throughout the world that are seeking to please the Lord, not the consumer, and that draw their marching orders from Scripture and not from the culture. Some reacting to the seeker-model will head for these churches and be discipled according to biblical principles. Others, such as some of the very people that King and Kimball represent, will be attracted to elements of spiritual formation. Much of what has been discussed so far in previous chapters concerning spiritual formation has to do with private or personal practices. While contemplative prayer and *lectio divina* can be elements of public worship, they are best experienced in solitude and silence. But for the movement to be valid it also needs a public dimension and presence. For those imbibing in spiritual formation concepts and techniques, public worship is most likely to be an adoption of liturgical practices found within Roman Catholic and Eastern Orthodox traditions. This is only logical given that spiritual formation is rooted in those traditions and being guided by them to this day. As a result, worshippers at evangelical churches are increasingly discovering icons, Stations of the Cross, incense, rosaries, prayer ropes and candles, more prevalent liturgy, and the liturgical year.

Many Protestants are unfamiliar with these methods and formats and simply believe their church leadership has come up with creative new ideas to augment worship. But the fact is these are not new ideas at all but ancient ones that go back to the early days of the church. In fact, it is the historic roots of these practices that are touted as reasons the church should embrace these methods today. The idea is that since these procedures and forms have deep roots in church history and because they were supposedly invented by "spiritual masters," we would be wise to incorporate them into our public and private worship today. It should be observed, as we examine some of these liturgies and methods, that most of them have no basis in Scripture. They have been invented by men and accepted by certain church hierarchies but they are not biblically-based. As a result, at the very least none of these practices should be seen as mandatory for spiritual growth or church life. Let's overview some of the things spiritual formation is incorporating into its system for worship.

The Liturgical Year

Phyllis Tickle, general editor of the eight volume "Ancient Practices Series" for publisher Thomas Nelson believes it is the liturgy and the liturgical cycle that binds the faith community together and "deepens our understandings of what it means to live more fully, more deeply, more spiritually from year to year."[150] Joan Chittister, the author of *The Liturgical Year*, one of the books in "The Ancient Practices Series," states, "The liturgical year is the arena where our life and the life of Jesus intersect."[151] When our lives intersect with that of Jesus great things are promised.

Like the voices of loved ones gone before us, the liturgical year is the voice of Jesus calling to us every day of our lives to wake our sleeping selves from the drowsing effects of purposelessness and meaninglessness, materialism and hedonism, rationalism and indifference, to attend to the life of

Jesus who cries within us for fulfillment. Then the world will change. Then the people will be saved. Then the reign of God promised by Jesus, preached by the apostles, and proclaimed by the lives of the saints will have come. Then life will be what is meant to be: the love of God fully alive in us.[152]

This a tall order. Can adherence to the liturgical calendar really deliver on all these promises? If so then the very fact that much of Protestantism has neglected the liturgical year may be the reason that the world has not changed, salvation is not more prevalent, the kingdom of God has not fully come and life is not all it was meant to be. If all of this is true, we certainly want to be on board. But before we jump on, let's take a brief look at the specifics of the liturgical year. Robert Weber, the father of the "Ancient-Future Movement", which overlaps with the spiritual formation views under discussion, informs us,

The Christian year, which developed in the first few centuries of the church, marked yearly time by Advent (waiting for the Messiah), Christmas (the Messiah has come), Epiphany (the Messiah is manifested to be for the whole world), Lent (preparing for the death of Jesus), Holy Week (reenacting the final week and saving events), Easter (celebrating the resurrection), Ascension (Jesus ascends in glory to intercede for us at the right hand of the Father), and Pentecost (the coming of the Holy Spirit in a new way).[153]

As can readily be seen, the liturgical calendar celebrates or commemorates the most important events in the Christian faith; there is no argument with this. But within the liturgical system very precise liturgies and structures have been developed by which these events are to be remembered. According to Chittister there are four major kinds of celebration: Sundays; seasons of the year such as Advent, Christmas, Lent and Easter; the sanctoral cycle commemorating the lives of certain saints; and Ordinary Time—the two periods of time between Eastertide and Advent, and then again between Christmastide and Lent.[154] Within these four major kinds of celebrations are numerous minor celebrations. For example there are four feasts of Ordinary time: Trinity Sunday, Corpus Christi, the feast of the Sacred Heart, and Christ the King.[155] There are also 16 events dedicated to Mary each year.[156] Add to these all the many other celebrations, solemnities, feasts and memorials and the church calendar gets pretty full. Let's take a closer look at just two of these celebrations:

Lent

Lent is the word used to denote the forty-day fast preceding Easter. In modern times it is usually observed from Ash Wednesday to Maundy Thursday (approximately six weeks). Its traditional purpose is to prepare believers for Easter through various forms of prayer and sacrifice. During Lent many will participate in selective fasts or abstinence from luxuries or some types of food. Chittister covers Lent in her chapter entitled "Asceticism" and says, "Lent revolves around sacrifice ... We must be prepared to give up some things if we intend to get things that even are more important."[157] Lent draws from the asceticism of early monasticism,

> Ardent Christians, monastics, left the cities where narcissism held full sway to live as solitaries in the desert in order to do battle with the enemies of the soul. They practiced harsh penances and purged themselves completely of all worldly pleasures in order to witness to a life beyond this life, a life beyond the gratification of the body to the single-minded development of the soul.[158]

Chittister is happy that the extremes of asceticism are a thing of the past; nevertheless, she applauds the goal of the ascetics which "is to conquer themselves and develop their souls."[159] Asceticism is the idea that by putting our physical bodies through deliberate suffering and hardship we will master our inward passions. It is "through acts of asceticism, we learn the most difficult thing in life: we master the gift of self-conquest. We are no longer prey to our own excesses. Now we are in control of the most difficult material we'll ever confront—ourselves."[160] The problem with asceticism is both that it doesn't work and more importantly, it is unbiblical. Paul clearly torpedoed the whole ascetic movement when he wrote in Colossians 2:20–23,

> If you have died with Christ to the elementary principles

of the world, why, as if you were living in the world, do you submit yourself to decrees, such as, "Do not handle, do not taste, do not touch!" (which all refer to things destined to perish with use)—in accordance with the commandments and teachings of men? These are matters which have, to be sure, the appearance of wisdom in self-made religion and self-abasement and severe treatment of the body, *but are of no value against fleshly indulgence.*

Deliberate asceticism, harsh treatment of the body and abstinence from acceptable activities, actions and food, may have the appearance of spiritual activity but have no effect on our souls, nor do they enhance our spiritual development. Lent is a hold-over from ascetic practices of the past that have no direct spiritual value.

Marian Piety

While not everyone involved in spiritual formation will be devoted to Mary, it cannot be ignored that Mary is front and center in the liturgical year. Chittister affirms that Marian theology is "the DNA of religion in our bones ... Marian piety is part of the roots of the church. It is not only part of the most ancient devotions in the church; it has a continuing and present power ... The Marian liturgical tradition is one of the pillars of the church."[161] With this backdrop it is no wonder, as previously noted, there are fully 16 events on the liturgical calendar dedicated to Mary. Those who want to follow the liturgical calendar, and yet filter out Mary, are going to have a difficult task. She is at the very heart of ancient liturgy.

Authority

Before moving on, it is important to address the issue of authority. By what authority have the liturgical year and liturgical practices been established? It is one thing to develop and keep an optional tradition that is neither obligatory nor universally acclaimed as spiritually beneficial; it is another to make certain practices and traditions both mandatory and necessary for spiritual growth. For example, I like the tradition of Thanksgiving. I observe it and enjoy it, but it is not mandated by the church nor is there any particular spiritual enhancement I receive from gathering with family and friends and overeating. But the liturgical year with its celebrations, feasts and traditions are all backed by the authority of the Catholic Church and seen as absolutely essential for spiritual formation (see Chittister's remarks above). But wait a minute: we have at least two problems. Not all who promote liturgical living agree. Eastern Orthodoxy, for example, has a very different liturgy that some believe is far superior to the Catholic one. For example Robert Webber, a strong proponent of liturgical living, claims that "the style of Roman worship is much more legalistic and rigid" than in Orthodoxy.[162] Further, "Eastern and Western worship differed in content, structure, and style. The content of Eastern worship maintained a strong resemblance to the narrative of ancient worship, emphasizing creation, incarnation, and re-creation in the pattern of Word and sacrament. Western worship, on the other hand, reduced the full content of God's story to a focus on the sacrifice of Christ for sin."[163]

So which liturgy is the right one? By what authority do we make such decisions? This brings us to the second and real issue. No one who champions spiritual formation and/ or the liturgical year makes any claims that these practices, traditions and liturgies are found in Scripture. Chittister, for example, is clear that every aspect of the liturgy and the liturgical year is rooted in extrabiblical sources and developed years after the close of the New Testament, often centuries later.[164] This is not a problem to one steeped in Catholic theology (since final authority rests in the Church's magisterium), but it is a problem for those in Orthodoxy who have their own magisterium, and even a bigger problem for those who confess *sola Scriptura*. For the latter the final authority is found in the revelation of God as found in Scripture. The Bible does not tell us to follow a liturgical year or perform certain liturgies in order to be growing followers of Christ. Therefore, the teachings of Scripture on the subject of discipleship are being pushed aside and replaced by the teachings of men, something Jesus condemned in no uncertain terms (Matthew 15:1–9).

Sabbath Keeping

Another book written in the Ancient Practices Series is *Sabbath*. It was written by Dan Allender, founder of Mars

Hill Graduate School (recently changed to The Seattle School of Theology to avoid confusion with Mars Hill Church), to promote Sabbath keeping as a spiritual discipline. Allender develops three core premises in this book:

- The Sabbath is not merely a good idea; it is one of the Ten Commandments. Jesus did not abrogate, cancel, or annul the idea of the Sabbath.

- The Sabbath is a day of delight for humankind, animals, and the earth; it is not merely a pious day and it is not fundamentally a break, a day off, or a twenty-four-hour vacation.

- The Sabbath is a feast day that remembers our leisure in Eden and anticipates our play in the new heavens and earth with family, friends, and strangers for the sake of the glory of God.[165]

It is important to note that Allender does not draw any of his premises from Scripture but rather from Jewish tradition, ancient and modern practices, and rituals created and imagined by Allender and those in his mystically-oriented camp.[166]

For example, Allender claims that since Sabbath is part of the Ten Commandments Christians are to keep it. Not only does this ignore the frequent New Testament statements proclaiming us free from the Mosaic Law and the fact that Sabbath-keeping is never commanded in the New Testament for the church, but Allender also has no intention of actually following the prescribed Old Testament manner in which Sabbath was kept. Working from Deuteronomy 5:12–15, which states Sabbath as a day of rest, Allender immediately twists the passage to teach Sabbath as a day of play and celebration of creation.[167] At no point does the author mention, nor does he intend to apply, the many and stringent Old Covenant regulations regarding Sabbath. Instead, Allender makes an inexplicable leap from the pages of Scripture to an imaginary understanding of Sabbath as a day of pretense and delight.

In order to delight in Sabbath, Allender recommends many options from lighting candles, smoking pipes, drinking good wine, finger painting, taking a hike, reading a novel, fly fishing (even if it is an imaginary adventure on the lawn), and eating the best of food.[168] The only stipulation is that Sabbath must be pursued with delight: "What intrigues, amazes, tickles your fancy, delights your senses, and casts you into an entirely new and unlimited world is the raw material of Sabbath."[169]

Not only is Sabbath a day of play, it is also a day of pretense. "It is a day we pretend that all is well, our enemies are not at war with us, and the peace we will one day enjoy for eternity, is an eternity that utters this day on our behalf."[170] Sabbath then "is a fiction,"[171] a day lived as if there was no sin, a day of "curiosity, coziness, and care."[172] It is a party.[173] We are to pretend and play on Sabbath as if the new heavens and earth were here.[174] Such pretense will require props which could include candles, using our finest china, or rituals such as "Sabbath sex" or a walk in the woods.[175]

In other words, Allender has created a totally novel and unbiblical view of the Sabbath, one that would be completely unrecognizable by Old Testament Jews as well as church age Christians. He has not drawn his concepts from Scripture, nor has he made any serious attempt to do so. He is content with the opinions of his peers, his own imagination and the direct communication that he receives supposedly from the Lord.[176] In short *Sabbath* is a work of fiction, not exactly the kind of fiction Allender recommends but fiction nevertheless.

I have based my impression of spiritual formation leaders's view on the Sabbath keeping on Allender's book because I think it is fairly representative of others who want to incorporate the Sabbath into spiritual formation. Allender is admittedly more extreme than many others, but of those pushing for some form of Sabbath keeping, virtually no one is recommending keeping it as it was prescribed under the Old Covenant. When Christian leaders latch onto an idea or concept and then depart from biblical teachings to promote their own imagination they have become their own authority. This will always lead to errant living.

Icons, Rosaries, and Stations

One of the criticisms of the worship services of many Protestant/evangelical churches is that they are too cerebral. "Talking heads" (preachers) are attempting to reach their audience almost exclusively through the ear-gate, and musicians take a similar approach. In contrast, Dan Kimball believes, "Emerging generations desire a multisensory worship experience" in which all the senses are addressed.[177] He writes, "God created us as multisensory creatures and chose to reveal himself to us through all of our senses."[178] For those like Kimball who accept this presupposition, the best place to turn for multisensory experiences is the ancient practices and traditions created by the Catholic and Orthodox Churches. Mike King states, for example, "Over two thousand years of church history, believers have developed practices, disciplines and ways to be conformed into the likeness of Christ."[179] Some worship practices gleaned from past tradition (but notably not from Scripture) and increasingly found in Protestant churches today are the use of icons, praying the rosary or prayer ropes, Stations of the Cross, making the sign of the cross and the daily office. We will briefly look at three of these.

Icons

The use of icons in the worship of God has long been a lightning rod and a source of much controversy and division within historic Christianity. Images of God are strictly forbidden in the Ten Commandments, but Catholicism came to see icons as windows between earthly and spiritual worlds. Richard Foster tells us that John of Damascus (d. 749) provided a clear theology for the use of icons in Christian devotions.

> He taught, in summary, that before God took human form in Christ, no material depiction was possible and therefore blasphemous even to contemplate. Once God became incarnate, however, depiction became possible. Since Christ is God and part of the triune Community, it is justified to hold in our mind the image of God incarnate. Hence, because of the incarnation of Christ, using physical images of Jesus becomes part of a full incarnational, or enfleshment, theology.[180]

Foster believes "the seventh ecumenical council of 787 settled the matter for the Christian community by affirming the use of icons and other symbols as a valid aspect of Christian worship. In expressing this conclusion, the council was careful to make a clear distinction between the veneration of icons and the worship of icons."[181] Mike King wants to make it evident that he does not pray to icons, but he prays *with* icons and says he has "experienced some profound encounters with God while praying with icons."[182] Regardless of what was decided at the Second Council of Nicaea in 787, or what is being experienced by King, there is not a hint of the use of icons to worship the Lord in either Testament. The Old Testament clearly condemns the use of icons and the New Testament does not change the command of God. In addition the early, apostolic New Testament churches do not make any use of them. Someone might counter that the New Testament does not mention pews or church buildings either, but we use them today. However, the Bible does not condemn pews or church buildings, as it does images of God, and neither is directly used in worship in the same way icons are.

Rosary and Prayer Ropes

The Rosary is a long standing Catholic tradition aimed primarily at the veneration of Mary. As an individual fingers the Rosary beads he prays certain prayers that make up the rosary including repeated sequences of the Lord's Prayer and ten "Hail Mary(s)" and one praying of "Glory be to the Father."

The prayer rope is a necklace-like loop often made of wool which serves a similar purpose as the rosary within the Orthodox tradition. It consists of fifty to a hundred complicated knots, the purpose of which is to count the number of times the Jesus Prayer is prayed.

Stations of the Cross

It is becoming popular for evangelical churches to use the Stations of the Cross in their worship services or for special events, especially during Passion Week. The Stations of the Cross are a set of fourteen stations used to represent the final hours of Christ beginning when Jesus was condemned to death and culminating with His burial. The participant moves physically from station to station meditating on what Christ did at each point represented by that particular station. It is therefore a prayer pilgrimage based upon chief scenes of Christ's sufferings and death. It has been popular within Catholic worship for centuries. Some believe the incorporation of the Stations into public worship began with Francis of Assisi and gained popularity throughout the Medieval period. At each Station there would be icons or pictures to aid in meditation. As with many of the other practices found in Catholicism and Orthodoxy, and now being adopted by some within the Spiritual Formation Movement, there is neither biblical precedent nor instruction for the use of the Stations. Some are entirely imaginary, such as the station in which Veronica is giving Jesus water.

Conclusion

The "face" of the Spiritual Formation Movement, as well as contemplative spirituality and emergent Christianity, is often first noticed within evangelical churches by the incorporation of traditional Roman Catholic and Eastern Orthodox practices and liturgies. Many of these practices are being introduced at special events and eventually find their way into the regular services of the church. Worshippers are often confused by what they are experiencing and do not understand what is taking place. It should be understood that when traditions borrowed from errant groups such as Catholics and Orthodoxy are taken into evangelical worship and life, and are done so without a careful examination of

Scripture, what is being adopted is more than just methods. There is a comprehensive, and in many ways wrong, theology upon which these practices rest. Methods do matter, and we are naïve to think that we can take techniques from false religions and not eventually embrace their theology.

6

Ignatius's Spiritual Exercises

One of the most popular and strongly promoted activities within spiritual formation is known as "The Spiritual Exercises of Ignatius Loyola." As the name implies, these are exercises or activities invented by the Roman Catholic monk Ignatius of Loyola in the 16th century to enhance spiritual life, first his own and then that of the monks within his monasteries. The exercises are complicated and difficult, and were practiced almost exclusively by Catholic monks for almost 500 years until the birth of the modern Spiritual Formation Movement in the latter part of the 20th century. Today there is no doubt more interest in the exercises than at any other point in history. To grasp Ignatius's Spiritual Exercises, we will begin with a short history of Ignatius, including the society of monks he founded, move to the original 16th century exercises as found in Ignatius's book, examine their modern application especially among Protestants, and then discuss why the Exercises are of deep concern to lovers of biblical Christianity.

History

Ignatius was born into a wealthy Spanish home in 1491. As a Catholic living during the time of the Reformation, he found himself facing some of the most religiously turbulent times since Constantine. Trained to be a knight, he joined the Spanish army and, in May 1521, at the Battle of Pamplona while fighting against France, he was hit by a cannonball and sustained major damage to his legs. While recovering he spent much time reading spiritual literature which led him to leave behind his life of wealth and live as a hermit. He devoted himself to asceticism and the example of others of like mind, such as Francis of Assisi. In 1522, while living in a cave and practicing extreme asceticism, he claimed to have seen visions of the Virgin Mary and the baby Jesus which radically changed the course of his life. Shortly thereafter he began to pen the Spiritual Exercises. In 1539, he and a few friends established the Society of Jesus, better known as the Jesuits, to aid in the Catholic struggle against the Reformation. Ignatius and the Jesuits became a leading force in what became known as the Counter-Reformation, which began at the Council of Trent (1545–1563) and continued until 1648, when the Thirty Years' War came to an end. This was Rome's attempt to counter or turn back the Protestant Reformation through decrees, education, or force, including war.

As the Jesuits became better organized, Ignatius eventually became their Superior General, a position he would keep until his death in 1556. He spent much of his life in monastic settings and devoted himself to furthering the cause of the Pope (the Jesuits dedicated themselves to God and to the Pope) through education, missionary endeavors and attempting to lead the Counter-Reformation.

The Original Spiritual Exercises

Ignatius is best remembered today for two things—founding the Society of Jesus and inventing the Spiritual Exercises. It is his Exercises that have had significant influence on Protestants in recent years through their adoption and promotion by leaders in the Spiritual Formation Movement. Perhaps the best way to understand the Exercises is to turn to an official source such as the Jesuits's Oregon Providence. Its website states,

> Spiritual Exercises of St. Ignatius of Loyola are a month-long program of meditations, prayers, considerations, and contemplative practices that help Catholic faith become more

fully alive in the everyday life of contemporary people. It is set out in a brief manual or handbook: sparse, taciturn, and practical. It presents a formulation of Ignatius' spirituality in a series of prayer exercises, thought experiments, and examinations of consciousness—designed to help a retreatant (usually with the aid of a spiritual director) to experience a deeper conversion into life with God in Christ, to allow our personal stories to be interpreted by being subsumed in a Story of God.[183]

The following brief summary is helpful in understanding both the purpose and mythology of the Exercises:

The Spiritual Exercises of St. Ignatius form the cornerstone of Ignatian Spirituality—understanding and living the human relationship with God in the world exemplified in the Society of Jesus (Jesuits). Although originally designed to take place in the setting of a secluded retreat, during which those undergoing the exercises would be focused on nothing other than the Exercises, in his introductory notes, Ignatius provides a model for completing the Exercises over a longer period without the need of seclusion. The Exercises were designed to be carried out while under the direction of a spiritual director. Spiritual Exercises were never meant only for the vowed religious. Ignatius of Loyola gave the Exercises for 15 years before he was ordained, and years before the Society of Jesus was even founded. After the Society was formed, the Exercises became the central component of the Jesuit novitiate training program, and they usually take place during the first year of a two year novitiate.[184]

The aim of Spiritual Exercises seems to be to enable people to know God better and aid them in their walk with the Lord, but the book itself is extremely confusing and virtually incomprehensible in places. Modern adaptations, as we will see below, use the skeleton behind Ignatius's book but depart rather significantly in application. The reason for this is that *Spiritual Exercises* is not a coherent, organized piece of writing. It is more like a collection of ideas, prayers, meditation and rules. Nevertheless Ignatius clearly divides his exercises into four parts, or weeks, each period of time focusing upon a different theme:

First, the consideration and contemplation on ones sins;

Second, the life of Christ our Lord up to Palm Sunday inclusively;

Third, the Passion of Christ our Lord;

Fourth, the Resurrection and Ascension, with the three Methods of Prayer.[185]

As a person works his way through the exercises, hopefully with a friend or better a spiritual director, his goal is to better be able to discern God's will for his life and draw closer in fellowship with the Lord. *The Exercises*, which Ignatius first wrote in 1522 and continued to revise until 1548, were essentially a set of rules designed to train those who desired to become Jesuits. As a matter of fact, the book is full of rules: rules for the discernment of spirits, rules for making good decisions, rules for eternal salvation and peace, rules to put oneself in order for the future, rules for the distribution for alms, rules to develop a militant church, rules for thinking, rules for eating and drinking, rules of education, rules to explain images, rules for secrecy, and on and on. The rules, as well as much of the book are very Roman Catholic, as one might expect. To give a flavor of how *The Spiritual Exercises of Ignatius* read, I will quote 13 of the 18 rules found under the heading, "To have the true sentiment which we ought to have in the church militant:"

First Rule: All judgment laid aside, we ought to have our mind ready and prompt to obey, in all, the true Spouse of Christ our Lord, which is our holy Mother the Church Hierarchical.

Second Rule: To praise confession to a Priest, and the reception of the most Holy Sacrament of the Altar once in the year, and much more each month, and much better from week to week, with the conditions required and due.

Third Rule: To praise the hearing of Mass often, likewise hymns, psalms, and long prayers, in the church and out of it;

likewise the hours set at the time fixed for each Divine Office and for all prayer and all Canonical Hours.

Fourth Rule: To praise much Religious Orders, virginity and continence, and not so much marriage as any of these.

Fifth Rule: To praise vows of Religion, of obedience, of poverty, of chastity and of perfections of supererogation. And it is to be noted that, as the vow is about the things which approach to Evangelical perfection, a vow ought not to be made in the things which withdraw from it, such as to be a merchant, or to be married, etc.

Sixth Rule: To praise relics of the Saints, giving veneration to them and praying to the Saints; and to praise Stations, pilgrimages, Indulgences, pardons, Cruzadas, and candles lighted in the churches.

Seventh Rule: To praise Constitutions about fasts and abstinence, as of Lent, Ember Days, Vigils, Fridays and Saturday; likewise penances, not only interior, but also exterior.

Eighth Rule: To praise the ornaments and buildings of churches; likewise images, and to venerate them according to what they represent.

Ninth Rule: Finally to praise all precepts of the Church,

keeping the mind prompt to find reasons in their defense and in no manner against them.

Tenth Rule: We ought to be more prompt to find good and praise as well the Constitutions and recommendations as the ways of our Superiors. Because, although some are not or have not been such, to speak against them, whether preaching in public or discoursing before the common people, would rather give rise to fault-finding and scandal than profit; and so the people would be incensed against their Superiors, whether temporal or spiritual. So that, as it does harm to speak evil to the common people of Superiors in their absence, so it can make profit to speak of the evil ways to the persons themselves who can remedy them.

Eleventh Rule: To praise positive and scholastic learning. Because, as it is more proper to the Positive Doctors, as St. Jerome, St. Augustine and St. Gregory etc. to move the heart to love and serve God our Lord in everything; so it is more proper to the Scholastics, as St. Thomas, St. Bonaventure, and to the Master of the Sentences, etc., to define or explain for our times the things necessary for eternal salvation; and to combat and explain better all errors and all fallacies. For the Scholastics Doctors, as they are more modern, not only help themselves with the true understanding of the Sacred Scripture and of the Positive and holy Doctors, but also, they being enlightened and clarified by the Divine virtue, help themselves by the Councils, Canons and Constitutions of our holy Mother the Church.

Twelfth Rule: We ought to be on our guard in making comparison of those of us who are alive to the blessed passed away, because error is committed not a little in this; that is to say, in saying, this one knows more than St. Augustine; he is another, or greater than, St. Francis; he is another St. Paul in goodness, holiness etc.

Thirteenth Rule: To be right in everything, we ought always to hold that the white which I see, is black, if the Hierarchical Church so decides it, believing that between Christ our Lord, the Bridegroom, and the Church, His Bride, there is the same Spirit, which governs and directs us for the salvation of our souls. Because by the same Spirit and our Lord who gave the Ten Commandments, our holy Mother the Church is directed and governed.[186]

As can be seen, since these rules would have little to offer those not deeply involved with the Roman Catholic Church, why are they making such inroads within Protestant circles in recent times? The answer is that those in the Spiritual Formation Movement are largely borrowing the concepts offered by Ignatius and modernizing them to fit twenty-first century Protestant audiences.

Modern Application

We now move forward to see how the Exercises are being adapted and adjusted for a new audience who are mostly Protestant, usually evangelical, and who are unfamiliar with the ways and language of Roman Catholicism in general and Reformation-era terminology and ideas in particular. James Wakefield, a strong proponent for the Exercises and author of *Sacred Listening, Discovering the Spiritual Exercises of Ignatius Loyola*, claims that "*the* Spiritual Exercises *are an invitation to renew and deepen our relationship with Christ* ... [they] are primarily a series of meditations on the Gospels that help us clarify and deepen our commitments to Jesus Christ."[187] This certainly sounds inviting until we dig deeper. Before we do it should be noted that there are many who agree with Wakefield. Let's take a look.

Promoters of Ignatius Exercises

Virtually everyone connected with the Spiritual Formation Movement recommends the use of the Ignatius Exercises. Leighton Ford, formerly connected with the Billy Graham Evangelistic Association, recommends ending the day with an exercise known as the "examen" which "was recommended by Ignatius in his Spiritual Exercises, [and] because it helped to change him from a soldier to a pilgrim walking to Jerusalem."[188] Richard Foster points to the *Exercises of Ignatius of Loyola* as "disciplines of the spiritual life for training in righteousness."[189] Bruce Demarest, in conjunction with his recommendation of the use of imagination in meditation, writes, "The Spiritual Exercises of St. Ignatius employ the imagination and have been widely used for centuries as an aid to biblical meditation. At the heart of the Ignatian method is *the use of sensory imagination to engage biblical events* at a deeper and more personal level."[190] Mark Yaconelli claims, "In my own study I've found Ignatian or imaginative contemplation to be particularly effective in helping young people come in contact and conformity with the person of Jesus Christ."[191] Mike King uses the Exercises in his personal retreats.[192] Gregory Boyd writes, "I and many others have found Ignatius's *Spiritual Exercises* to be the most powerful tool for helping us grow in our walk with God."[193] And Eugene Peterson states, "The task of every Bible reader is to become a Bible *listener* so that we can start *living* the text. Ignatius of Loyola's *Spiritual Exercises* is one of the most influential guidebooks for directing us in listening."[194]

Ruth Haley Barton, who has written many books on spiritual formation themes and leads the Transforming Center which specializes in spiritual formation, recommends use of the Exercises in developing discernment. She writes,

> Discernment is first of all a habit, a way of seeing that eventually permeates our whole life. It is the journey from spiritual blindness (not seeing God anywhere or seeing him only when we expect to see him) to spiritual sight (finding God everywhere, especially where we least expect it). Ignatius of Loyola, founder of the Jesuits and best known for developing a set of spiritual exercises intended to hone people's capacity for this discipline, defined the aim of discernment as "finding God *in all things* in order that we might love and serve God in all."[195]

The Exercises for Modern Protestants

As far back as 1984, the Navigator's Discipleship Journal was reporting that the *Spiritual Exercises* were "a great spiritual classic."[196] Shortly thereafter James Wakefield, a Lutheran pastor and professor of biblical and spiritual theology at Salt Lake Theological Seminary, began to consider how he might adapt the Spiritual Exercises for use by Protestants who lacked the supervision from a trained Roman Catholic spiritual director. If you have read Ignatius's original book, or even the selections given in this chapter, you will quickly realize that in their original form the Exercises would be virtually unworkable by Protestants and even by most Catholics outside the monastic system. The result of Wakefield's efforts to "update" and make the Exercises more user friendly was eventually his book *Sacred Listening, Discovering the Spiritual Exercises of Ignatius Loyola.*[197] Wakefield claims that the "Spiritual Exercises are an invitation to renew and deepen our relationship with Christ … [and] are primarily a series of meditations on the Gospels that help us clarify and deepen our commitments to Jesus Christ."[198]

Wakefield breaks Ignatius's four weeks of spiritual exercises into four movements:

- The first movement has as its purpose to create a space within us that the Lord can fill, better known in mystical literature as purgation. The first unit of eight, under the first movement, is to introduce the reader to contemplative prayer which has been discussed in detail in an earlier chapter in this book. Contemplative prayer is an imaginative method of praying that is never found or endorsed in Scripture, but is at the heart of all forms of mysticism. Specifically the form of contemplative prayer that is introduced is that of *lectio divina*,[199] which is an imaginative form of praying the Scriptures also explained earlier in chapter two of this book.

Wakefield offers a number of opportunities to practice the Exercises drawn from Ignatius. One example concerns hell where we are told to use our imagination and take a journey to hell describing what we see, hear, taste, feel, and smell. [200]

In the original book Ignatius elaborates, "Ask for interior sense of pain which the damned suffer, in order that, if, through my faults, I should forget the love of the Eternal Lord, at least the fear of the pains may help me not to come into sin." We are, with our imagination to see "the great fires, and the souls as in bodies of fire; to hear with the ears wailing, howlings, cries, blasphemies against Christ our Lord and against all His Saints ... to smell with the smell the smoke, sulphur, dregs and putrid things ... to taste with the taste bitter things, like tears, sadness and the worm of conscience ... to touch with the touch; that is to say, how the fires touch and burn the souls."[201]

Of course nothing remotely similar to this exercise is taught or recommended in Scripture and such imaginings are clearly dangerous. Perhaps for this reason Ignatius warned that the material found in the next three movements may not be useful and could actually be harmful to some people.[202] I would agree, but add that the first movement is equally as dangerous.

- The second movement is concerned with imaginatively contemplating scenes in the four Gospels. It is during this movement that Wakefield claims, "In weeks to come, it is common for the Holy Spirit to move you into deeper forms of contemplation as you spend longer times of silence during your prayer time."[203]

- In the third movement the imagination is shifted to the Passion of Christ. The second and third movements combined seek communication from Christ that is often termed illumination in mystical circles.

- The fourth movement determines to strengthen our attachment to Christ through imaginative meditations on the resurrection. This movement is to lead to the fourth stage of mysticism, that of union in which one is united in some mystical fashion to God. If someone reaches this stage he needs to be warned by Ignatius and Wakefield that "many disciples experience an odd phenomenon: they encounter a significant dry spell. They feel as though all consolation has left them, and they are somewhat numb."[204]

Dangers

There are a number of dangers in the use of *Ignatius's Spiritual Exercises* including elevating a man-made system for spiritual growth and development above the actual teachings of Scripture themselves. Then there is the complication of the system. It is no wonder that the Exercises are to be used with a Spiritual Director. Left to oneself, it would be virtually impossible to navigate through all the rules and imaginative projects that Ignatius offers.

But the primary danger is through the use of imagination the participant actually believes the Lord is speaking to him in some subjective form beyond the pages of Scripture. Wakefield says, "We need to focus closely on listening to the Holy Spirit throughout the process ..."[205] just as "Ignatius's own listening led to the development of these Exercises."[206] This should be more of an indictment than a commendation. It was Ignatius's imagination that caused him to develop this clearly man-made, unbiblical approach to spiritual formation. Where might our imagination, untethered to Scripture, lead us?

Read uncritically, *Ignatius's Spiritual Exercises* is little more than a program for spiritual discipline combined with devotional study of Scripture. Unfortunately it is much more than that. Besides its evident danger in regard to mystical practices, which opens the door to even more contemplative concerns, there is a subtle but obvious error. Throughout the book Scripture is used in an imaginative way. That is, a passage is read not to gain understanding but to engage the text with imagination. The goal is not cognitive knowledge followed by healthy, reasonable application, but emotional involvement. This in itself is troublesome, but to add insult to God's Word we are offered an alternative—the "resources" of Ignatius.[207] These resources include Ignatian "Rules for Discernment," as well as Ignatian "Principles and Foundation" ("Kingdom Exercises," "The Two Standards," "Three Classes of People," "Three Kinds of Humility," and a prayer called "Take, Lord"). These resources form the instructional (cognitive) material which is supposedly used to guide the participant into "holiness." In this process, the Scriptures become a mere by-product, utilized to engage the imagination. It was Ignatius's teachings that actually became the foundational material for the adherents of the Exercises. Ignatius's word, therefore, supersedes God's Word. We should take seriously the words of Jesus in Matthew 15:9: "But in vain do they worship me, teaching as doctrines the precepts of men."

7

Discernment and Revelation

Discernment, one would think, is an extremely positive quality. In a world in which there are incalculable numbers of voices calling us to travel many different directions, discernment is invaluable. However, when used by those involved in spiritual formation, discernment is defined as the discipline that enables one to know when a person has supposedly heard the voice of God. Spiritual formation leaders do not question that God speaks to us today apart from Scripture, but they do believe that since God is speaking there has to be a means whereby we can discern the voice of God from our own thoughts. Adele Ahlberg Calhoun writes in her *Spiritual Disciplines Handbook*, "Discernment opens us up to listen to and *recognize the voice* and patterns of God's direction in our lives."[208] Ruth Barton further explains,

> Discernment is a quality of attentiveness to God that is so intimate that over time we develop an intuitive sense of God's heart and purpose in any given moment. We become familiar with God's voice—the tone, quality and content—just as we become familiar with the voice of a human being we know well.[209]

Christian psychologist Larry Crabb believes he has learned the art of listening to God and proposes to let us in on what he has discovered in his book *The Papa Prayer*, "Sometime, though never audibly, I hear the Father speak more clearly than I hear the voice of a human friend."[210] And influential pastor John Ortberg adds, "It is one thing to speak to God. It is another thing to listen. When we listen to God, we receive guidance from the Holy Spirit."[211]

As we contempt the subject of discernment it is important that we determine whether or not God does speak to Christians today outside of the Scriptures themselves. This is hardly an issue pertinent only to the Spiritual Formation Movement. As a matter of fact modern day revelations (or lack thereof) from God are one of the most hotly debated topics within evangelicalism today.

Despite the fact that the majority of conservative evangelical Christians since the Reformation have held to a cessationist (that present day revelations from God no longer take place) position with regard to Divine revelation, true cessationists are rapidly disappearing. In the articles and books I have written nothing has evoked as much criticism and anger as my position that God is speaking authoritatively to His people today exclusively through Scripture. Due to the influence of a multitude of popular authors, theologians and conference speakers, cessationism is barely treading water, even within the most biblically solid churches and organizations. As a matter of fact, among those who claim to be evangelicals there are five identifiable views prevalent today on the matter of revelation:

Identifiable views:

- *Pentecostal/Charismatic/Thirdwave*: All miraculous gifts exist today, including the gift of prophecy. God speaks through prophets and to His people both audibly (through dreams, visions, words of knowledge), and inwardly (inaudibly in the mind or heart). Representatives of this position are Jack Deere, John Wimber, the Kansas City Prophets, the Assemblies of God and the Word of Faith movement. Charismatic author Tommy Tenney, in his popular book *The God*

Chasers, writes, "God chasers ... are not interested in camping out on some dusty truth known to everyone. They are after the fresh presence of the Almighty ... A true God chaser is not happy with just past truth; he must have *present* truth. God chasers don't want to just study the moldy pages of what God has done; they are anxious to see what God is doing."[212]

- *Classical Mysticism/Spiritual Formation:* Through the use of various disciplines and spiritual exercises, God will speak to us both audibly and inaudibly. Dallas Willard and Richard Foster are two such examples. Willard, a leader within the Spiritual Formation Movement, recently updated a previous book renaming it *Hearing God, Developing a Conversational Relationship with God.* The thrust of his book is that we can live "the kind of life where hearing God is not an uncommon occurrence, [for] hearing God is but one dimension of a richly interactive relationship and obtaining guidance is but one facet of hearing God."[213] In other words, the maturing Christian should expect to hear the voice of God on a regular basis, independent from Scripture, and that voice will reveal God's individual, specific will for his life. Such personal communication from the Lord, we are told, is absolutely essential because without it there can be no intimate walk with God.[214] And it is those who are hearing from God today, in this way, who will redefine "Christian spirituality for our time."[215]

- *Evangelical Mysticism*: God is speaking to Christians regularly, mostly inaudibly through inner voices, hunches, promptings, feelings and circumstances (examples: Henry Blackaby and Beth Moore). Southern Baptists ministers Henry and Richard Blackaby wrote *Hearing God's Voice* to "teach God's people not only to recognize his voice but also immediately to obey his voice when they heard it."[216] They promise that "as you spend time with Jesus, you will gradually come to recognize his voice more readily than you did at first … You won't be fooled by other voices because you know your Lord's voice so well."[217] And, once you have figured out when God is speaking to you, "write it down in a journal so you can refer back to it as you follow him."[218]

In this category could be placed the New Calvinists or Calvinistic Charismatics such as John Piper,[219] Wayne Grudem, Mark Driscoll and C. J. Mahaney. Their followers are sometimes called the young, restless, and Reformed. Mark Driscoll, who often claims extra-biblical revelation, dreams, and visions from the Lord, documented four such events in his recent book *Real Marriage*. He writes, "… when God spoke to me, I had never experienced anything like that moment. God told me to devote my life to four things. He told me to marry Grace, preach the Bible, train men, and plant churches. Since that day in 1990, that's what I have been pursuing by God's grace."[220] Mark Chandler would be on page with this idea. In his popular book *The Explicit*

Gospel Chandler writes, "He [God] speaks to us in dreams and in visions and in words of knowledge—but in no way that runs contrary to Scripture."[221] Long time Southern Baptist pastor, Charles Stanley is of the same opinion. In a recent interview with *Christianity Today* he is asked about his frequent references to God speaking to Him. He responded by mentioning a time that very week when God said to him, "Don't do that." He claims that he does not hear an audible voice "but it's so crystal sharp and clear to me, I know not to disobey that."[222]

Another prominent individual to add to this list is Sarah Young. Her devotional books *Jesus Calling* and *Jesus is Calling* are among the bestselling books in the world today. Young writes,

> I had been writing in prayer journals for years, but that was one-way communication with me through the Bible, but I yearned for more. Increasingly, I wanted to hear what God had to say to me personally on a given day. I decided to listen to God with pen in hand, writing down whatever I believed He was saying. I felt awkward the first time I tried this, but I received a message … My journaling had changed from monologue to dialogue. Soon messages began to flow more freely, and I bought a special notebook to record these words. This new way of communicating with God became the high point of my day. I knew these writings were not inspired as Scripture is, but they were helping me grow closer to God.[223]

- *Cessationist*: All miraculous gifts, including prophecy, have ceased (examples: the IFCA International, John MacArthur and Charles Ryrie). The Westminster Confession states well the historic cessationist position,

> The whole counsel of God concerning all things necessary for His own glory, man's salvation, faith and life is either expressly set down in Scripture, or by good and necessary consequence may be deduced from Scripture: unto which nothing at any time is to be added, whether by new revelations of the Spirit, or traditions of men.[224]

- *Cautious, but Open*: Those holding this position are skeptical of prophetic claims and the majority of inaudible experiences. But they do not want to "put God in a box" and therefore are cautiously open to the possibility of additional revelation from the Lord today, although they are not certain how this works or how to identify God's voice. Nevertheless, they are afraid to limit the power of God and fear that they might be missing out on a close personal relationship with the Lord if they do not allow for the possibility of God speaking today apart from Scripture (examples: most Christians).

Modern Revelations

Continuationists, those who believe that the miraculous sign gifts, including prophecy, are still available to believers today, define their supposed revelations in different ways. There are

two broad categories that could be acknowledged, the first
of which claims prophetic messages from the Lord. Such
messages would be direct, clear words from God or angels,
perhaps in dreams or visions or through audible voices.
Such claims have long been common in Pentecostal and
charismatic circles and are increasing among non-charismatic
evangelicals. Extremely popular conference speaker and
author Beth Moore is well known for her claims of hearing
from God. In a DVD she states, "Boy, this is the heart of our
study. This is the heart of our study. Listen carefully. What
God began to say to me about five years ago, and I'm telling
you it sent me on such a trek with Him, that my head is still
whirling over it. He began to say to me, 'I'm going to tell
you something right now, Beth, and boy you write this one
down and you say it as often as I give you utterance to say
it.'"[225] Such statements coming from evangelicals are far too
common to need much documentation. Moore is claiming a
direct word from the Lord that sets the future agenda for her
ministry. The source of authority is her own experience.

From a more doctrinal base we turn to theologian
Wayne Grudem, who has had a massive impact on the
evangelical world concerning modern prophecies. Grudem
has written the definitive book on the subject, *The Gift of
Prophecy in the New Testament and Today*, in which he claims
that church age prophecy is different than Old Testament
prophecy. While the Old Testament prophet was held to
the standard of infallibility when speaking a word from the

Lord (Deuteronomy 18:20–22), prophecies beginning with
Pentecost are fallible and imperfect. He writes, "Prophecy in
ordinary New Testament churches was not equal to Scripture
in authority, but simply a very human—and sometimes
partially mistaken—report of something the Holy Spirit
brought to someone's mind."[226] Modern prophecy then is
impure and imperfect. By way of example and documentation
Grudem quotes the Anglican charismatic leaders Dennis and
Rita Bennet who claim,

> We are not expected to accept every word spoken through
> the gifts of utterance ... but we are only to accept what is
> quickened to us by the Holy Spirit and is in agreement with
> the Bible ... one manifestation may be 75% God, but 25% the
> person's own thoughts. We must discern between the two.[227]

One of the most disconcerting aspects of Grudem's position
is his uncertainty as to how we can distinguish between our
own thoughts and those supposedly from God. This is such
an important and disturbing feature of the conservative
continuationist's system that I will quote Grudem at length.

> But how would a person know if what came to mind was a
> "revelation" from the Holy Spirit? Paul did not write specific
> instructions; nonetheless, we may suppose that in practice
> such a decision would include both an objective and subjective
> element. Objectively, did the revelation conform with what

the prophet knew of the Old Testament Scriptures and with apostolic teaching?[228]

With this quote cessationists partially agree. The Holy Spirit cannot contradict Himself and anything allegedly spoken by the Holy Spirit which is in disagreement with Scripture is naturally spurious. The continuationists, however, are rarely claiming new doctrines that supplement Scripture; they are claiming specific, personal words that guide them in decision making or knowledge of the future. It should be mentioned in passing that contrary to what is often stated by continuationists, many espousing modern prophecies do in fact add numerous doctrines not found or taught in the Bible such as specific demonic warfare techniques, insights on heaven or hell, "word of faith" authority that releases the power of God, dominion theology, novel views on the atonement, inspiration and ecclesiology. While more conservative continuationists such as Grudem, Piper, and Mahaney would not be guilty of such theological additions, many others are.

Turning back to Grudem we read of his subjective element of prophecy,

> But there was no doubt also a subjective element of personal judgement: did the revelation "*seem like*" something from the Holy Spirit; did it *seem* to be similar to other experiences of the Holy Spirit which he had known previously in worship

… Beyond this it is difficult to specify much further, except to say that *over time* a congregation would *probably* become more adept at making evaluations of prophecies, and individual prophets would also benefit from those evaluations and become *more adept* at recognizing a genuine revelation from the Holy Spirit and distinguishing it from their own thoughts.[229]

When we contrast Grudem's view of prophecy with Scripture we find nothing remotely resembling what Grudem teaches. Nowhere in the Bible is one receiving a message from God left to wonder if God is speaking to him (with the temporary exception of the young boy Samuel). No one had to ask if what they were hearing "seemed like" the Holy Spirit or matched previous subjective experiences that also "seemed like" the Holy Spirit. They knew without question when God was speaking to them. This is essentially the same teaching that Dallas Willard exerts in *Hearing God*: "How can you be sure God is speaking to you? The answer is that we learn *by experience*."[230] Therefore subjective experience becomes the test of authority concerning revelation from God. This is a far cry from what we find in Scripture.

The second half of Grudem's quote moves into the realm of the incredible. After 2000 years of church history, the best this world-class theologian can offer is that "over time a congregation would probably become more adept at making evaluations of prophecies …" This is a statement of speculation and hope that at some point the church will begin to figure out when a word of revelation is actually coming from the Holy Spirit and when it is the imagination of the speaker.

Let's put Grudem's hypothesis to a test. Sister Sally stands up in church and says the Holy Spirit has just revealed to her that an earthquake will flatten much of the city sometime within the next eight weeks. The congregation needs to add earthquake insurance to their properties, pack all their belongings, leave their jobs behind and head to the countryside. What is to be done? Given Grudem's theory, the congregation knows that at best this prophecy is impure and most likely contains elements that are not from God. The people are then left to evaluate the validity of the revelation just received based on their own experience or other purely subjective means. In the Bible, if a true prophet of God warned of an impending earthquake there would be no doubt as to what to do, but Grudem's New Testament prophet is unreliable. I have to ask, of what value is such a prophecy? It has no authority or certainty, and may actually lead to bad and even disastrous decisions. These modern prophecies do not have the ring of "thus says the Lord."

An excellent example of the unreliability and danger of these sorts of modern prophecies is found in a recent interview with highly respected pastor and theologian John Piper. Piper admits,

A woman came to me, while my wife is pregnant with my fourth child. And she says, "I have a very hard prophecy for you." I said, "OK." She says—in fact she wrote it down and gave it to me—"Your wife is going to die in childbirth and you're going to have a daughter." I went back to my study—I thanked her, I said, "I appreciate that." I forget what I said but it wasn't—, I didn't want to hear that, I went back to my study, I got down and I just wept ... And when we delivered our fourth boy, not girl, I gave a "whoop," which I always do, but this whoop was a little extra; because I knew as soon as the boy was born this was not a true prophecy.[231]

When the different views on modern revelation and prophecies collide, continuationists attempt to pacify cessationists by assuring them that their messages from the Lord are not on par with Scripture. Grudem quotes George Mallone saying,

Prophecy today, although it may be helpful and on occasion overwhelmingly specific, is not in the category of the revelation given to us in the Holy Scripture ... A person may hear the voice of the Lord and be compelled to speak, but there is no assurance that it is pollutant-free. There will be a mixture of flesh and spirit.[232]

Since almost no one within Christianity (save the cults) is claiming revelation that is equivalent to the Bible, we are left with a dilemma. Is it possible for God to speak in a non-authoritative way? Is it possible for Him to speak something less than His inspired word? The continuationists seem to have invented a novel type of divine revelation; one that contradicts Scripture and defies reason. In the Bible, and logically, either God is speaking or He is not. There is no such thing as partially inspired revelation or the true words from the Lord polluted by the misunderstanding or imagination of the prophet. This is not to say that all of God's divine words are found in Scripture. John is careful to inform us that Jesus did many things, and certainly said many things, that are not recorded in his Gospel (John 20:30), or the other New Testament books for that matter. Yet all that Jesus said were the words of God. He never expressed an impure or untruthful thought. He spoke with authority. Undoubtedly the Spirit also spoke through various men and women in biblical times whose words were not recorded in the Bible. The point, however, is that, while the Holy Spirit has not included every prophecy that He spoke through humans in Scripture, everything that He inspired people to say carries with it the infallible authority of the Word of God. Nothing that He said through people is less than God's word. A polluted or partial revelation from the Holy Spirit has never been uttered.

This means that modern prophecies, words of knowledge, and other claims to hearing the voice of the Lord, if they are truly from the Holy Spirit, must be equal to the Scriptures in both inspiration and authority. God cannot speak with other than purity and inerrancy. Modern claims of the Lord speaking but with a "mixture of flesh and spirit" simply are not possible and are never attested to in Scripture. Those who are claiming divine revelation today must wrestle with the fact that what they are supposedly hearing must carry the same authority of the divinely inspired authors of Scripture.

A Case for Cessationism

With all of this as a backdrop, the question is reduced to this: Is God giving authoritative revelation on par with that which He has given in the past, much of which has been inscripturated, or is He not? If He is, then the church of Christ needs to take note and come into compliance with the modern prophecy movement, following its revelations as it would Scripture. But if the Lord is not revealing His inspired word today, then we need to reject the claims of the modern prophets and expose these supposed revelations for what they are. This means the position taken by most on prophecy—cautious but open—is untenable. The cautious but open crowd is skeptical of the claims coming from the prophetic movement and they are suspicious of the many "words from God" that so many evangelicals are claiming. Still they hesitate to embrace cessationism. They are concerned about limiting God or, as it was mentioned above, "putting God in a box." To this let me make two replies:

- It is okay to put God in a box if God, in fact, is the One who put Himself in that box. In other words, God can do anything He wants to do, but we expect God to do what He says He will do. For example, could the Lord take away the salvation of one of His children? Of course He could—He is sovereign. But He has promised He will not do so, so He won't. The Lord has put Himself in that box. Could the Lord flood the earth again? Certainly, He is omnipotent. But He has promised not to do so, so He will not. He has placed Himself in that box. Similarly, If God has put Himself in the cessationist box we can embrace and proclaim it.

- Taking the open but cautious view really does not hold up. Either God is speaking today apart from His Word or He is not. If He is speaking, how do we determine which of the multitude of messages people claim are from Him and which are bogus? If, with Grudem, we have eliminated the tests of Deuteronomy 13 and 18, how are we to evaluate all these revelations? How do we know to whom we should listen and whom we should ignore?

On such an important area as divine revelation it is indefensible to believe that God's people cannot know with certainty whether such is taking place. Surely we should expect that the Scriptures themselves would lay out the guidelines for us to determine if divine, authoritative, inspired revelation is being given today. I believe it does and that we can be confident, from the witness of Scripture itself, that God has ceased speaking to mankind during this age apart from the Bible. Let's take a quick look at what the Word has to say.

A cessationist view begins with a careful look at what God actually did in Scripture. We find, when we search carefully, that God was not speaking to everyone all the time. His revelation, even in biblical times, was rare and when He did speak it was always supernaturally with an audible voice, never through inner voices or impressions. The assumption held by many that God spoke to most of His children in biblical times is simply not true. The average believer in either Testament never received a personal word from God and even the majority of key players never heard the voice of God personally. When God did speak in Scripture it almost always dealt with the big picture of what He was doing in the outworking of His redemptive program or the life of His people in general. You will search in vain to find God instructing someone to take a job, purchase a number of donkeys, or buy a house—except as it related to the bigger issue of God's dealings with His people. Beyond a few individuals, finding a non-prophetic person in Scripture who heard directly from God becomes a difficult task. The contention that God spoke to almost everyone all the time, leading, guiding and directing, simply does not stand the test of careful examination of the Scriptures. Even those to whom God spoke in the Old Testament, to only Noah, Abraham, Moses (considered to be a prophet), Jacob, Aaron, Joshua,

David and Solomon, did He speak more than twice in their
lifetimes.

But what about the New Testament? We find that most
records of God speaking to individuals after Pentecost are
found in the book of Acts. But even here we find only
thirteen distinct times in which God spoke directly to
individuals (two of these through angels), (8:26–29; 9:4, 10;
10:3, 11–16; 12:7–8; 13:2–4; 16:6,9–10; 18:9; 21:4, 11; 22:17–21;
23:11). Eight of these occasions were to Paul or Peter, leaving a
total of five other individuals or groups to whom God spoke
directly in the first 30 years of church history.

So far, we have examined what might be called negative
evidence. That is, if we are looking for a pattern of how God
spoke to individuals in scriptural times, that pattern reveals
a scarcity of individual revelations. The Lord chose to speak
primarily through His prophets and the apostles. Following
that pattern we should expect the same today. Let's now move
to more positive evidence that the Lord has ceased speaking
today apart from Scripture.

Beginning with Ephesians 2:20, we find that the church
is "built on the foundation of the apostles and prophets."
Since Christ is the cornerstone of the church, this verse has
to be speaking of the witness concerning Christ that the
apostles and prophets provided to the church. It is only to be
expected that this witness would be passed along to the future

generations of believers via the instrument of Scriptures that those men were inspired to write. As Ephesians 3:5 tells us, the "mystery of Christ" has been "made known to the sons of men through the revelation given to Christ's holy apostles and prophets." In the next chapter, Paul teaches that the Lord has provided gifted men to the church for its perfection or maturity (Ephesians 4:11–16). The apostles' and prophets' role in that process was laying the foundation of the church, as we have seen (Ephesians 2:20; 3:5). How? Through the teaching of New Testament truth, the apostles' doctrine. The early church gathered together to devote "themselves to the apostles' teaching" (Acts 2:42), for it was the apostles who would provide New Testament revelation, as it was handed down to them by the Lord Himself (Matthew 28:19–20) and through the inspiration of the Holy Spirit (2 Timothy 2:2; 3:16).

The book of Hebrews enhances our understanding by detailing two periods in human history in which the Lord has spoken to mankind. Hebrews 1:1 proclaims that the first period was "long ago to the fathers and prophets in many portions and in many ways." This is an obvious reference to the revelations given during the times of the Old Testament. In verse two the author of Hebrews cites the second period of divine revelation by simply saying that "in these last days [God] has spoken through His Son." But as we know Jesus Himself did not write down anything that He said. That was left to His followers and so, the author of Hebrews adds:

"After it was first spoken through the Lord, it was confirmed
to us by those who heard" (Hebrews 2:3) i.e. the apostles. This
however raises a practical problem. How did the people know
that the communication they were receiving from the apostles
was true? After all, many individuals made claim to being an
apostle during the first century. The Lord would authenticate
His true apostles by giving them the ability to perform "signs
and wonders, and by various miracles and by gifts of the Holy
Spirit" (Hebrews 2:4). When the Corinthians challenged
Paul's apostleship and authority, he pointed them to the
"signs of a true apostle ... [which were] signs and wonders
and miracles" (2 Corinthians 12:12), just as the author of
Hebrews confirmed. The book of Acts verifies repeatedly that
miraculous gifts were taking place through the apostles for
this very reason (Acts 2:43; 5:12, 13; 9:38–41; 14:3, 8–9; 15:12;
19:11; 20:10; 28:8, 9). The only exceptions were Stephen (6:8),
Philip (8:6–7) and possibly Barnabas (15:12), all very closely
associated with the apostles. We find no examples of the
average Christian in the New Testament either performing
miracles or receiving authoritative revelation. Miracles were
for the purpose of authenticating the office of the men who
would lay the foundation of the church. Once the foundation
of the church was in place, the role of the apostles was
no longer needed. With the death of John, the last of the
apostles, gifts authenticating the apostles were no longer
necessary and they ceased.

But did that necessarily mean revelation ceased as well? I

believe the evidence of Scripture would indicate that it did. We start with 1 Corinthians 13:8–10, which clearly tells us that the day comes when prophecy and supernatural knowledge will be done away, and tongues will cease. Specifically Paul writes that "when the perfect comes the partial will be done away." All Bible believers are ultimately cessationists for this passage is clear that revelatory knowledge will cease at some point; that point being when the perfect comes. Many believe that the "perfect" refers to the coming of Christ or the eternal kingdom. That is a possible interpretation but the context is contrasting partial knowledge and revelatory gifts with that which is perfect. The best explanation in such a context would be that the perfect (or complete) would be the completion of Scripture. In other words, when the revelation for this dispensation as recorded in the New Testament is completed the need for partial words of knowledge and prophecies would cease. That is, because the final, full revelation of the Lord for this dispensation has arrived, there is no need for additional messages from God. This seems reasonable, but did it happen?

Apparently so, for this understanding of the perfect in 1 Corinthians 13 is reinforced later in the New Testament by Peter, Jude, Paul and John. When the apostle Peter pens the inspired epistle we call Second Peter, he is desirous of reminding them of many things, especially that they "remember the words spoken beforehand by the holy prophets and the commandment of the Lord and Savior spoken by your apostles" (3:2). Peter did not point his readers to new or fresh revelation but to the words spoken previously by the prophets and apostles. Jude offers similar understanding when in verse three he urges his readers to "contend earnestly for the faith which was once for all handed down to the saints." A message had been given, a foundation laid once for all that had to be defended. How did they know what that message was? In verse 17 Jude answers, "But you, beloved, ought to remember the words that were spoken beforehand by the apostles of our Lord Jesus Christ." The faith in verse three that was handed down to them, the faith that was to be defended and proclaimed, had been given to them by none other than the apostles.

As the apostle Paul writes virtually his last inspired words to his friend Timothy he points him to the Scriptures that are able to make the people of God "adequate, equipped for every good work" (2 Timothy 3:16–17). In light of this lofty claim for the God-breathed Scriptures, Paul gives Timothy a final charge—"to preach the word …" (4:1–5). There is no hint in Paul's charge that Timothy is to seek additional revelation, listen to the prophecies or words of knowledge of fellow believers or preach his own dreams or visions. He is to preach the Word handed down to the saints through the apostles. As the New Testament canon nears its close the divinely inspired authors unite in pointing their readers to the apostles as the inspired human source of New Testament truth.

The apostle John joins the chorus as he closes down the New Testament with a solemn warning against adding to or subtracting from this final revelation from God. He writes, "I testify to everyone who hears the words of the prophecy of this book: if anyone adds to them, God will add to him the plagues which are written in this book; and if anyone takes away from the words of the book of this prophecy, God will take away his part from the tree of life and from the holy city, which are written in this book" (Revelation 22:18–19). Since this is the last chapter in the last book of the last Testament it is only reasonable to deduce that from that point on any addition of any prophecy would be adding to Scripture. With the death of John shortly thereafter, the last of the apostles had faded from the scene and with him the final word of revelation for this age. In addition there is no indication either the twelve apostles or the New Testament prophets were ever replaced (Revelation 21:14).

The witness emerging from the Scriptures themselves is that God has chosen to communicate with mankind throughout history in specific and unique ways. He has chosen certain men at certain times to be prophets and apostles to speak and record divine revelation (Hebrews 1:1–2; 2:3–4). When God's revelation was complete for this age, the ministry of the prophets and apostles was finished and we would expect no further communication at this time. This expectation is verified through the statements found in the Bible itself. What we are seeing today is not new revelation from God but subjective experiences and, at times, deception. Let us cling tenaciously to "the faith which was once for all handed down to the saints" (Jude 3) rather than chasing the inferior, inadequate imaginations of those who claim a new word from the Lord today.

8

Fasting and Spiritual Direction

The list of spiritual disciplines that has been adopted within the Spiritual Formation Movement is almost endless. We could analyze the divine office, Benedict's Rule, use of the Rosary and prayer ropes, monasticism, journaling, the Eucharist, and pilgrimage, among many others. But we will conclude our study of the disciplines with fasting and spiritual direction.

Fasting

Of course fasting is not a practice unique to spiritual

formation. Christians of all theological stripes have fasted since the inception of the church, and the Old Testament saints, not to mention those of pagan religions, made fasting part of their religious life. In order to get a handle on fasting it would be good to break our study into three parts: what spiritual formation leaders teach about fasting, how fasting is understood within more evangelical circles, and what the Bible says on the subject.

Spiritual Formation and Fasting

Dallas Willard tells us that "fasting is one of the more important ways of practicing that self-denial required of everyone who would follow Christ (Matthew 16:24). In fasting, we learn how to suffer happily as we feast on God."[233] Willard offers a quote from Thomas à Kempis to support his views: "Whosoever knows best how to suffer will keep the greatest peace. That man is conqueror of himself, and lord of the world, the friend of Christ, and heir of Heaven."[234] Willard makes clear what he is trying to say in this summary statement:

> Persons well used to fasting as a systematic practice will have a clear and constant sense of their resources in God. And that will help them endure deprivation of *all* kinds, even to the point of coping with them easily and cheerfully. Kempis again says: "Refrain from gluttony and thou shalt the more easily restrain all the inclination of the flesh." Fasting teaches

temperance or self-control and therefore teaches moderation and restraint with regard to *all* our fundamental drives.[235]

The idea Willard is promoting is that fasting is a means of sanctification. Through practicing this discipline we suffer deprivations that train us to curb our appetites, control our flesh and conform us to Christlikeness. Through the discipline of fasting we can expect spiritual growth and formation. We will examine the idea that fasting is a means of sanctification later, but for now it is significant to note at this point that Willard draws his conclusions without reference to Scripture and what God tells us about the purpose of fasting. Rather his primary resource appears to be the Roman Catholic mystic, Thomas à Kempis. When we turn to Richard Foster he rightly remarks that "there simply are no biblical laws that command regular fasting."[236] He points to the ancient Christian devotional book the *Didache* instead, which prescribed fasting on Wednesdays and Fridays, and John Wesley's revival of these teachings among early Methodists.

Scot McKnight writes a whole book for "The Ancient Practices Series" simply entitled *Fasting*. McKnight contends that fasting is merely the natural, inevitable response of a person to a grievous or sacred moment (such as sorrow or spiritual desire) which may or may not lead to a desired result or benefit. He states that "fasting is not an instrument that can be utilized to get what we want,"[237] yet when he fleshes out reasons for fasting he lists: to help us become more compassionate, to gain clarity, to be a blessing, to grow spiritually, to draw closer to God, to develop love for God and others, to overcome temptation, or to get answers to prayer.[238] While McKnight admits that the Bible gives very limited instruction on fasting[239] he believes fasting is vital for today based on Old Testament Jewish practices and the witness of church history. "Who are we," he questions, "to neglect what God's people have always done?"[240] He does admit, however, that ancient Jews in response to grievances or sacred moments also wore sackcloth, pulled out their hair, tossed dust on their head and tore their clothing, in addition to fasting.[241] Who are we, I might ask in turn, to pick and choose which of these ancient practices to incorporate into our Christian life while rejecting others? McKnight, just as Willard and Foster, is crafting a doctrine of fasting by cherry-picking from examples found in Scripture, Jewish and church history, rather than developing an understanding from the Scriptures themselves.

Other spiritual formation leaders could be referenced but it would result in mere redundancy since they all follow a similar line of reasoning. Therefore, we want to move on to the teachings of those who represent more mainstream views of evangelicalism.

Evangelicalism and Fasting

A well-respected evangelical church in Chicago often calls for days of prayer and fasting. In a published brochure the following is offered to the church members to encourage them to join in a fast:

> Fasting is a full-body response to God. However, it is not a substitute for obedience nor is it a way to manipulate God. It is a sign of our desperation and a deep desire for complete repentance with an accompanying hunger for God. Richard Foster says, "More than any other discipline, fasting reveals the things that control us. This is a wonderful benefit to the true disciple who longs to be transformed to the image of Jesus Christ. We cover up what is inside of us with food and other things." Let us obey this Scripture, "Consecrate a fast; call a solemn assembly. Gather the elders and all the inhabitants of the land to the house of the Lord your God, and cry out to the Lord" (Joel 1:18).

This shows clearly how many understand the role of fasting today as well as the in-roads that spiritual formation leaders have made into mainline evangelical churches. While we could consult reams of books and articles on fasting throughout the ages, I want to turn to the well-known evangelical theologian and pastor John Piper for his views, which I think epitomize those of many evangelicals. I will be drawing from his book *A Hunger for God, Desiring God through Fasting and Prayer* to document Piper's understanding of the role of fasting in the life of the Christian.

He states early that "the birthplace of Christian fasting

is homesickness for God" (p. 13). Additionally Piper makes numerous and powerful claims for fasting. He believes: it awakens our appetite for God (p. 23); it will help keep us from turning gifts into gods (pp. 17–20); fasting is a test to see what desires control us (pp. 19, 58); it is an intensifier of spiritual desire (p. 22); we cannot face the hazards of life and ministry without fasting (pp. 51, 62–63); Jesus triumphed over the devil by fasting and, thus, we owe our salvation, in some measure, to fasting (p. 55); fasting is a physical expression of heart-hunger for the coming of Jesus (p. 83); it awakens us to latent spiritual appetites by pushing the domination of physical forces from the center of our lives (p. 90); the reason we do not fast is because we are content with the absence of Christ (p. 93); it was fasting in Acts 13 that changed the course of history (p. 107); and fasting is meant to starve sin (p. 136).

Piper quotes Martin Luther favorably as stating, "It is right to fast frequently in order to subdue and control the body. For when the stomach is full, the body does not serve for preaching, for praying, for studying, or for doing anything else that is good. Under such circumstances God's Word cannot remain."[242] And he adds a more concerning quote from John Wesley in which he says, "The man who never fasts is no more in the way to heaven than the man who never prays"[243]

As is obvious, Piper is a strong supporter of fasting, but he recognizes that Old Testament fasting is not the same as Christian fasting. The Old Testament people fasted primarily for two reasons: longing for the Messiah and mourning (over loss, danger or sin).[244] They also fasted on Mondays and Thursdays Piper states,[245] although he does not mention that this practice is found not in the Old Testament but in the Gospels and was part of the tradition of the Pharisees, not a scriptural mandate. Piper readily admits that there is no New Testament command to fast but he assures us that we must embrace fasting although not as was found under the Old Covenant. "We'll take it, but we'll change it," he writes.[246]

Piper's position on fasting faces a number of problems. First, despite the strong statements and claims for fasting mentioned above, none of them is supported directly by Scripture. For example, nowhere in either Testament are we told that fasting awakens our appetite for God, or helps us control our appetites, or intensifies our desire for God, or pushes the dominion of physical forces from our lives. The purpose for fasting was to grieve over sin and loss.

Secondly, in the absence of any command in the New Testament to fast, coupled with virtually no mention of fasting in the epistles and only two examples in Acts, Piper has to scramble to make a case for fasting during the church age. In addition there are strong arguments questioning the role of fasting for the Christian that must be handled. Piper hits these head-on and early. He opens his book by listing Scriptures that warn against asceticism (1 Timothy 4:13; Colossians 2:20–21; 1 Corinthians 8:8; Luke 18:12–14).[247] He then points to four objections that some have to Christian fasting: fasting is not uniquely Christian; the arrival of the kingdom negated the need for fasting; the danger of fasting in that it could lead to pride; fasting seems to be a denial of the joy of the indwelling presence of the Holy Spirit.[248]

Piper's reply to these concerns comes in three forms: examination of Scripture, testimonies of others, and personal conviction. The primary argument, of course, must be what the New Testament teaches and in this regard he sees Matthew 9:14–17 as the most important New Testament passage on fasting. Jesus' and His disciples did not fast, according to this text, because they were in the presence of the Bridegroom but when the Bridegroom is taken away Jesus declares "they will fast."[249] Piper rejects, as I would, that this future fasting by His disciples should be confined to the three days between the Cross and the Resurrection, so he concludes that Jesus must be referencing the church age in which His disciples will fast in His absence. Therefore, according to Piper, fasting should be a normal part of the Christian life (I will examine this line of reasoning in the next section).

The author uses a few other New Testament references to prove his case but none convincingly. He claims that 2 Corinthians 6:5 and 11:27 speak of Paul fasting[250] when clearly these verses are in the context of either forced hunger as one of the persecutions he suffered for the sake of the gospel, or voluntary absence from food because of the intensity of the immediate opportunities for ministry. Piper correctly points to Acts 13:1–3 and 14:23 to show that fasting was still practiced on occasion by the New Testament church but never addresses that at least a few of the Christians at the time, such as Paul, still participated in some Jewish feasts and rituals. If we are patterning our lives after examples, rather than direct instruction, why do we not as Christians keep the Jewish traditions as some of the apostles did for a time? What is lacking in Piper's exegesis is clear teaching or command in the New Testament Scriptures for church-age fasting. Examples might give us freedom to fast but they are not a mandate. Romans chapter 14 is an important text in regard to this subject but is not adequately addressed in this *A Hunger for God*. Quite frankly Piper does not prove his case for Christian fasting from the New Testament.

Piper's next line of argument is examples and quotes drawn from throughout church history. He devotes chapter five to such experiences and he ends *A Hunger for God* with an appendix of quotes favoring fasting. Of course, quotes and examples, while interesting, carry no authority if not backed by Scripture. But of even greater concern is that Piper draws from a number of disturbing sources. There are references to spiritual formation leaders such as Richard Foster and Dallas Willard,[251] Roman Catholic priests and monks, and the Desert Fathers and early church mystics from which much of modern fasting practices originate.[252]

Piper's final line of argumentation is his own conviction and authority. The claims he makes for fasting, earlier, simply cannot be proven by Scripture. They are the opinion of Piper and those who back his views. For example, when using Acts 13 as proof for Christian fasting he does not mention that the passage lacks specific reasons as to why this early church was fasting, and that nothing is said about their hunger for God that led them to fast.[253] This is typical of the book. Piper makes powerful claims for Christian fasting but he does not prove these claims from the New Testament.

One Old Testament text that the author spends much time on is Isaiah 58 which condemns Israel for keeping fasts while its heart was far from God. This is an excellent reminder, but Piper uses the passage to springboard into his belief in the Cultural Mandate (although not mentioned by name) that the church has been called to social action as part of the Great Commission (pp. 22, 127–153). Piper can make this link only by equating Old Testament Israel with the New Testament church. By doing so he does not distinguish life under the Old Covenant from New Testament teaching concerning life during the church age. This is foundational to Piper's position on fasting. The logic is that if fasting was an important part of Old Testament Israel's spiritual life then it must also be an important part of the Christian's life today. Piper believes that now during the church age we must make some changes and adjustments to Old Testament life, but we must not break the link to these things. It is on the basis of this theological premise that Piper can promote fasting so heavily in spite of the absence of New Testament teaching to back his views.

With some massaging and minor revision I believe Piper's views on fasting are representative of many, if not most, evangelicals who are promoters of the practice. A careful comparison between this view and that of the spiritual formation leaders will reveal only minor differences, if any. As can be seen in Piper's book, he even draws on some of the same authors, examples and quotes used by the Spiritual Formation Movement. What we must do now is turn our attention to Scripture and see what it has to say about fasting during the church age.

Biblical examination

The orthodox Jews of Jesus' day seemed to believe that self-induced discomfort enhanced their religious experience. It was for this reason that the Pharisees fasted twice a week—Monday and Thursday from sunrise to sunset, even though seemingly the only mandated fast in the Jewish calendar was on the Day of Atonement (Leviticus 23:26–32), and even that is not clear in the text. It is also true that in the Old Testament many of the Jewish leaders called for fasts for various reasons (e.g. 1 Samuel 7:6; 2 Chronicles 30:3; Joel 1:14 Ezra 8:21), however none of these fasts were made part of regular Jewish worship by the Lord, nor were they mandated by Jewish Law. Nevertheless the Pharisees added prescribed fasts, along with numerous other rituals to the point that their spiritual lives had become duty-laden drudges, filled with one unpleasant "have-to" after another and often motivated by fear.

When Jesus and His followers came on the scene they did not fit into the Pharisees' mold. Rather than fasting they feasted. Rather than have the appearance of mourning they exhibited joy, and these things irritated the Jewish spiritual leaders. These differences came to a head in Matthew 9:9–17 (Mark 2:14–22; Luke 5:27–38) when Jesus and His disciples were feasting at Matthew's house with "tax collectors and sinners." If this were not bad enough they were apparently feasting on one of the self-prescribed fast days of the Pharisees. The account in Mark reveals that the disciples of John the Baptist joined the Pharisees in their criticism of Jesus. Apparently John's disciples, while not embracing the hypocrisy of the Pharisees, had nevertheless accepted their view of piety and they too fasted twice a week. The joyful feasting of Jesus and His men, right in the face of those fasting, did not sit well. How could Jesus claim to be a spiritual man (at the very least) and not observe the twice weekly fasts?

Jesus knew that, in the case of the Pharisees, their religion was a show and a sham (Matthew 6:1–8). But on this occasion He does not address this, instead He tells them why He and his disciples are different. He uses a common illustration that they could all understand, an illustration about a wedding (Matthew 9:15). Weddings in the days of Jesus, as today, were times for feasting and joy, not times for fasting and mourning. According to William Barclay, during the first century, when two young people married in Palestine they did not go away for a honeymoon; they stayed at home and for a week they kept open house. They dressed in their best, sometimes they even wore crowns; for the week they were king and queen and their word was law. They would never have a week in their hard-wrought lives like that again. And the favored guests who shared this festive week were called the children (or sons, or attendants) of the bride chamber. During the week, when the bride and the groom were holding court, it was a time for joy and feasting. But the day would come soon enough when the wedding was over and they returned to the routine of life (Matthew 9:15b).

Jesus is obviously applying this illustration to Himself. He is the Bridegroom in the story and His disciples are feasting, not fasting, because Jesus was still with them and no one fasts when the bridegroom is still present. But the day was coming, at the crucifixion, when Jesus would be taken away. At that time the disciples' laughter would be turned into mourning, their joy to sorrow and their feasting to fasting. The question we must ask is what Jesus meant by the words, "those days?"

There is no doubt that "those days" include the days immediately following the crucifixion, and almost certainly they would include the time from the crucifixion to the coming of the Holy Spirit. But does it include the church age, as Piper contends? I don't think so. Consider that Jesus had promised His disciples that when He went away He would send the Holy Spirit (John 14:16, 17; 16:7) who would be another helper (Greek: Paraclete)—just like Him. As a matter of fact Jesus said that it would be to their advantage for Him to leave and send the Holy Spirit to them (John 16:7). It seems to me that the period of time between the crucifixion and the coming of the Holy Spirit to indwell the believers best fits Jesus' description of a time of mourning that would require fasting.

The issue is this: since the Holy Spirit has come and since we are again in the presence of the Bridegroom (in the form of the Holy Spirit) should not Christians rather rejoice than fast today? If Jesus' disciples avoided fasting and feasted instead in the presence of the Bridegroom, why should not the Christian do the same now that the Holy Spirit indwells him, especially in light of Jesus' promise that it was to our advantage that He go away and send the Spirit?

There are strong opinions on both sides of this issue. Some believe (as I have documented above) that fasting is the missing ingredient in the spiritual life of Christians today. If we would but fast as the Old Testament saints fasted we would know God's power in ways that we do not now. But as we examine Scripture pertaining to the church age we discover some interesting things. While fasting is never prohibited in the epistles, neither is it ever promoted. There is no instruction to fast and there are no prescribed fasts for the church. There are two examples of fasts in the book of Acts by the early church, but no mention that this was either the norm or expected of the churches. There are two, possibly three, mentions of fasting in the epistles. Second Corinthians 5:5 and 11:27 are covered above leaving only 1 Corinthians 7:5 where we find the word "fasting" added to "prayer" in the *Textus Receptus* manuscripts and inserted in translations that are based on that manuscript family (such as the KJV). Earlier manuscripts, upon which translations (such as the NASB and ESV) are based, do not include fasting, but even if it is the best rendering this does not change the New Testament understanding of fasting. First Corinthians 7 is in the context of the believers at Corinth adding unhealthy ascetic practices, in this case abstinence from marital intercourse, in the misguided understanding that doing so enhanced their spiritual life. Paul refuted this idea and called for normal, regular physical relationships within marriage, with the exception of mutually agreed upon short periods of time in order to devote themselves to prayer (and "fasting" if the *Textus Receptus* is followed). I personally have never known anyone to make specific application of this text, but it demonstrates the freedom we have in Christ to do so.

We must conclude, in the absence of either command or instruction in the New Testament concerning this subject, that fasting is not prohibited and therefore a believer is free to fast if he chooses. But since it is never commanded or even recommended for the church age we must assume that it is not a necessary ingredient for the Christian walk. As a matter of fact, fasting seems to be one of the areas specifically addressed by Paul to be a matter of personal conviction (Romans 14:5–9; Colossians 2:16–23). If you want to fast do so. But don't require it of others, or make it a test of spirituality, or expect it to aid in your sanctification. Jesus' emphasis was not on fasting, but on the joy of His presence. In the presence of Jesus, through the ministry of the indwelling Holy Spirit, who could not be joyful?

Fasting is neither commanded nor rejected in the New Testament, but left to the circumstances and convictions of individual Christians. It entered into the life of the ancient church through early uninspired Christian teachings (such as the *Didache)* and the church's slow but steady drift toward ritualism and mysticism. The only required fast in the Old Testament was possibly for the Day of Atonement and that has been fulfilled in Christ. And given that there are no commands or instruction in the New Testament for fasting it seems safe to say that fasting is not a requirement for Christians today. As a matter of fact, 1 Timothy 4:3 implies that advocating abstaining from foods which God has created is a sign of false teaching rather than a mark of spirituality. If Jesus and His disciples saw no need to fast, and if it is rarely mentioned following the Ascension and never promoted in the epistles, then surely it is not necessary today for spiritual growth. A quote from J. Oswald Sanders gives the proper balance: "Fasting is not a legalistic requirement but a spontaneous reaction under special circumstances ... There are ... godly and prayerful people who have found fasting a hindrance rather than a help ... There is no need for such to be in bondage. Let them do what most helps them to pray."[254] With this I agree.

Spiritual Direction

Spiritual direction and "trained" spiritual directors are all the rage these days. Richard Foster claims, "In our day, the desperate need is for the emergence of a massive spiritual army of trained spiritual directors."[255]

A general description of spiritual direction is:

The practice of being with people as they attempt to deepen their relationship with the divine, or to learn and grow in their own personal spirituality. The person seeking direction shares stories of his or her encounters of the divine, or how he or she is experiencing spiritual issues. The director listens and asks questions to assist the directee in his or her process of reflection and spiritual growth.[256]

This definition seems benign enough until one realizes that spiritual direction flows out of Roman Catholic contemplative spirituality. When Richard Foster wrote his

Celebration of Disciplines in 1978, he lamented that spiritual directors and direction was "hardly understood, let alone practiced, except in the Roman Catholic monastic system."[257] Foster believed this was a tragedy given what he calls its exemplary history: "Many of the first spiritual directors were the desert Fathers and were held in high regard for their ability to discern spirits."[258] Of course through the efforts of Foster, Dallas Willard, and a host of other spiritual formation authors and leaders, all of this has changed and spiritual direction is found throughout all branches of Protestantism and evangelicalism.

Today spiritual direction is a primary means of training people in the doctrines and disciplines of the Spiritual Formation Movement, but its main focus is in training people to hear and interpret the voice of God independently from the Scriptures. The Jesuit Press has a website entitled IgnatianSpirituality.com in which spiritual direction is clearly explained:

> Spiritual direction is "help given by one Christian to another which enables that person to pay attention to God's personal communication to him or her, to respond to this personally communicating God, to grow in intimacy with this God, and to live out the consequences of the relationship."[259]

- *Spiritual direction focuses on religious experience.* It is concerned with a person's actual experience of a relationship with God.

- *Spiritual direction is about a relationship.* The religious experience is not isolated, nor does it consist of extraordinary events. It is what happens in an ongoing relationship between the person and God. Most often this is a relationship that is experienced in prayer.

- *Spiritual direction is a relationship that is going somewhere.* God is leading the person to deeper faith and more generous service. The spiritual director asks not just "what is happening?" but "what is moving forward?"

- *The real spiritual director is God.* God touches the human heart directly. The human spiritual director does not "direct" in the sense of giving advice and solving problems. Rather, the director helps a person respond to God's invitation to a deeper relationship.[260]

As can be seen a spiritual director is not one who explains Scripture, advises people on their spiritual lives, or provides biblical insight. The task of the spiritual director is to help his directee discern the voice of God in order to determine where the Lord is leading him. This is a purely subjective attempt at unraveling what the directee thinks the Lord is saying to him, but it is a logical step in the spiritual formation system due to the difficulty that people have in discerning the supposed subjective inner voice of God. As Ken Boa, himself an advocate of spiritual directives, states,

It is possible for some personality types to develop a false supernaturalism by becoming immersed in an artificial experience. Thinking they are communing with God, they are really lost in themselves. This problem of self-delusion and misguided zeal can be corrected by a willingness to accept sound advice through spiritual direction.[261]

Boa is right up to a point. When people enter into the sphere of subjective spirituality in which they view their own thoughts and hunches as the very voice of God, and are attempting to interpret what God is saying and what direction He is leading, they often become confused and even self-deluded. Under this scenario terrible choices can be made. The spiritual formation solution to this serious problem is to follow the ancient Catholic method of spiritual direction. Unfortunately what this amounts to is adding another self-deluded person to the equation who will in turn attempt to help these confused people to discern the voice of God. The spiritual director, however, has no pipeline to God and can no more unravel the supposed direction from the Lord than those who have come to him for help. Rather than providing insight the spiritual director enters into the same subjective realm as his directee and faces the same impossible task of attempting to interpret a word from God that has never been given.

The Scriptures speak a great deal about helping one another in our Christian walk. Ephesians 4:15 calls on us to "speak the truth in love [in order that we] grow up in all aspects into Him who is the head, even Christ." But the context of this command is equipping the saints through the teaching of the Word of God. Paul tells Timothy to "be diligent to present yourself approved to God as a workman who does not need to be ashamed, accurately handling the word of truth" (2 Timothy 2:15). As Timothy understands the message of Scripture through this diligent study he is to entrust what he has learned "to faithful men who will be able to teach others also (2 Timothy 2:2). After reminding Timothy of the power of the inspired Scripture to both save and sanctify us (2 Timothy 3:15–17), Paul then charges him to preach the word and "reprove, rebuke, exhort, with great patience and instruction" (2 Timothy 4:2). Such biblical statements are multiplied many times over. We are to be involved in the lives of one another in order to strengthen the body of Christ and aid in its maturity so that we may live as He desires us to live (Ephesians 4:16). But the biblical pattern and instruction is not merely to listen to what people think God is telling them and subjectively lead them to determine which part of these supposed messages are really from God and which are not, as spiritual directors do. This is an act of futility and has no basis in Scripture whatsoever. Instead we are to minister to one another by helping people to discern and obey the infallible, objective and inspired word from the Lord as found in His Scriptures. We do not grow in Christ by contemplating our own thoughts, which we are attributing to God, but through the careful study and understanding of His inerrant Word.

Part Two
The Biblical Disciplines

The Spiritual Formation Movement, which we have now studied in detail in Part 1, claims to offer an almost unlimited number of spiritual disciplines that will aid in forming Christian character. While some of these have a bit of basis in Scripture, others have none, and even those which seems to be drawn, at least in part from the Bible, go beyond the Word in either their actually practice or what they promise or both. It is important to affirm that the word "discipline" is a good one and found in Scripture (e.g. Colossians 2:5). The issue is not whether discipline is helpful, even necessary for spiritual development—it is, for self-control is one facet of the fruit of the Spirit (Galatians 5:23). Nor do we wish to deny that there are

specific disciplines that aid in progressive sanctification. At
issue is what disciplines have actually been given to believers
as a means of discipleship? It is my firm conviction that any
means which the Lord has ordained for our use in the process
of spiritual growth would be identified in the Scriptures. If
the Bible is God's complete, authoritative revelation to us
today, and if it is designed to make us "adequate, equipped
for every good work" (2 Timothy 3:16–17), then we should
have every confidence that the inspired text would include,
with clarity, the instruments or means by which God would
have us grow. We do not need to reach beyond the written
Word to attempt to find practices for spiritual development
and intimacy with the Lord. The Lord is desirous that we
know these things and has made no effort to hide them
from us. It is not necessary for monks or hermits or other
spiritual leaders from the past (or present) to unearth some
secret formulas designed to teach us spiritual formation.
All that we need to know is found with certainty in God's
divine revelation, the Scriptures. This does not mean that
we cannot learn from fellow believers, we certainly can and
must. For example in 2 Timothy 2:2 Paul instructs Timothy
to take the very things Paul had taught him and teach them
to other faithful men, who in turn will teach others also. But
what Timothy was to pass on was not his own views and
experiences and visions but the truth of the Word of God as
given him by the inspired apostle (see 2 Timothy 1:13–14; 2:14;
3:10–4:5; Jude 17; Hebrews 2:3–4). The early church gathered
primarily to devote themselves to the apostles' teaching (Acts

2:42), not to study the supposed revelations of uninspired men and women. The body of Christ is essential in our spiritual development (Ephesians 4:11–16), but we aid that development as we "speak the truth in love" to one another (Ephesians 4:15). We also help one another with practical application of biblical truth. For example in Titus 2 older women are instructed to "encourage the young women to love their husbands, to love their children, to be sensible, pure, workers at home, kind, being subject to their own husbands, so that the Word of God will not be dishonored" (vv. 3–5). It should be noted that what the older women are to do by way of encouraging the younger women is to facilitate appropriation of truth already revealed in Scripture, not add ideas and revelations to Scripture.

When we turn to the Word of God to discover the Lord's clear teaching on discipleship what do we find? First, admittedly the Bible is a big book with many layers of wonderful truths about God, ourselves, the world, our future and more, waiting to be explored. It is a multi-faceted revelation from God, that reveals the wonders of Christ "in whom are hidden all the treasures and wisdom of God" (Colossians 2:3). This leads to perhaps the primary distinction between the Spiritual Formation Movement and biblical discipleship. Both camps would claim Colossians 2:3 for themselves and both would agree that it is in Christ that all the treasures and wisdom of God is hidden. The divide comes largely in the arena of revelation. Scripture promises believers

divine power which will grant "us everything pertaining
to life and godliness, through the true knowledge of Him
[Christ] who called us by his own glory and excellence"
(2 Pet 1:3). The question is, where is such knowledge of Christ
found? Is it found in the Holy Scriptures, or in extra-biblical
revelations and dreams, or both? As I argued in chapter
seven I believe that the only inspired revelation from God
for our times is the Bible. All other claims to revelations,
however sincere or well-intended, lack the authority of
Scripture. In addition, all other doctrines, methodologies,
philosophies, traditions, and spiritual practices that do not
emerge directly from the Word of God are at best suggestions
and opinions, some of which may be helpful, others not. But
when understood as having divine sanction these things fall
under the condemnation of Jesus who warned the Pharisees
that their traditions actually invalidate the Word of God
(Mark 7:13). Similarly Paul warned the Colossians, "See to it
that no one takes you captive through philosophy and empty
deception, according to the tradition of men, according to the
elementary principles of the world, rather than according to
Christ" (Colossians 2:8). The Spiritual Formation Movement,
as I have tried to demonstrate, has violated these principles
and "are teaching as doctrines the precepts of men" (Mark
7:7).

If so, it is time we turn our attention to what is actually
found in the inspired text pertaining to spiritual formation, or
the term I prefer, and I believe Scripture prefers, discipleship.

First, it should be stated up front that any effort on our part to produce Christ-like character is totally dependent upon the power of the Holy Spirit in our lives. Paul prayed for the Ephesians that "the eyes of your heart may be enlightened, so that you will know what is the hope of His calling, what are the riches of the glory of His inheritance in the saints, and what is the surpassing greatness of His power toward us who believe" (Ephesians 1:18–19). Later he continues, "That He would grant you, according to the riches of His Glory to be strengthened with power through His Spirit in the inner man ..." (Ephesians 3:16). Then in Philippians, immediately after telling these believers to "work out your salvation with fear and trembling" he follows up with, "For it is God who is at work in you, both to will and to work for His good pleasure" (Philippians 2:12–13). There is no growth in godliness without the power of the Holy Spirit. With this as a foundation, what are the means chosen and revealed by God, and energized by the power of the Holy Spirit, that the Lord has determined to use in our sanctification? If we are, through the energy of the Holy Spirit, to work out our salvation, how exactly are we to do so? Historically many Protestants have called these "means of grace," and the list has varied. Some see preaching the Word, baptism and Communion as the exclusive means of grace. Others would add prayer to the list. Still others would include the ministry of the body of Christ. And some would include anything that seems to be spiritual beneficial to the child of God.

I wish to narrow this list to what Scripture specifically identifies as the four means, or disciplines needed for spiritual growth. These can be summed up in the description given of the activities of the first church in Acts 2:42, 43a, "They were continually devoting themselves to the apostles' teaching and to fellowship, to the breaking of bread and prayer. Everyone kept feeling a sense of awe ..." These verses give us in a nutshell four essentials for spiritual development. We will examine each of these essentials, devoting one chapter to each. We will begin with prayer, followed by the indispensable study of the Word of God, then fellowship and finally the centrality of Jesus Christ and how He has chosen to transform our lives. These are the four essentials that I believe the Lord specifically affirms as means of spiritual formation: prayer, Scripture, the body of Christ and Christ-centered transformation.

9

Biblical Discipleship— Prayer

The Spiritual Formation Movement has rocked the church. This contemplative form of Christian spirituality, which has been detailed in the first section of the book, claims to offer an almost unlimited number of spiritual disciplines that will aid in forming Christian character. While some of these have a bit of basis in Scripture, others have none and even those which seem to be drawn at least in part from the Bible go beyond the Word in either their actual practice or what they promise or both. We now turn to the Word of God to see what it clearly teaches concerning disciplines necessary for spiritual maturity.

Views on Sanctification

Before we take a concise look at prayer it would be worth our time to discuss briefly some of the views of sanctification that have held sway within evangelicalism. The word "sanctification" comes from the Greek *hagios*. *Hagios,* and its many derivatives, is translated in the Bible as "sanctified," "sanctify," "sanctification," "holy," "saint" and so forth. The basic meaning of this word group is "to be set apart." In a purely secular sense, I could have a particular chair or cup that only I use and that chair or cup would be sanctified, set apart for my use only. Used in a spiritual context the word group speaks of being set apart for God, or for a holy purpose. The term is used in three tenses in Scripture, leading to three nuances of meaning. First, there is positional sanctification in which believers are redeemed from sin and set apart as the people of God (1 Corinthians 6:11). This is the believer's standing in God—it is who they are and it does not speak directly to how they live. At the moment of salvation we are set free from the penalty of sin and join the family of God. Sanctification also has an ultimate stage which takes place at the moment of the believer's death or the return of Christ (1 John 3:1–3). At that point we are set free from the presence of indwelling sin and are presented holy and blameless before the Father (Ephesians 5:26–27). A final way in which the word is used speaks of progressive sanctification in which the child of God grows more and more in his walk with the Lord (Romans 6:19; 1 Peter 1:16). It has been said that in positional sanctification the believer is set free from the penalty of sin; in progressive sanctification he is being progressively set free from the power of sin; in ultimate sanctification he is separated from the presence of sin. It is progressive sanctification which takes up the bulk of New Testament teachings as the Holy Spirit-inspired writers instruct disciples of Christ how to experientially live out their position in Christ while they wait for their ultimate holiness in the presence of the Lord. It is to this subject of progressive sanctification, or how the believer matures in Christ, that we now turn our attention. There have been a number of models held by various evangelical groups. They include:

Christian Perfectionism: Held by some in the Holiness, Pentecostal and Wesleyan camps, the idea is that at some point of spiritual crisis, whether a second work of grace or a second or even third baptism of the Holy Spirit, the sin nature can be eradicated and the believer can reach the point of sinlessness in this life.

Higher Life: Sometimes called Victorious Life, this view popularized by the Keswick Movement beginning in the mid-1800s also teaches a point of crisis in which the believer "lets go and lets God." At that moment the Christian realizes that he is to play a passive role in his spiritual development and rely upon God to do all that is necessary for sanctification.

Dedication: Formulated by Lewis Sperry Chafer in his book *He that is Spiritual*, it is argued that Christian growth comes as a result of being filled, or controlled, by the Holy Spirit. Through the power of the Holy Spirit the believer is enabled to obey the Lord and thus make significant progress in his spiritual walk. Chafer made a distinction between a Christian who is saved by grace and one who, at a moment of serious reflection, dedicates, or rededicates, his life to the Lord and is filled with the Spirit. Prior to this experience of dedication the believer will grow very little in the things of the Lord, but following the dedication the believer will mature in Christlikeness.

Spiritual Formation: Through the use of ancient spiritual disciplines Christ is formed in the life of the believer. The ultimate goal of spiritual formation is an event in which Christ is experienced in an inexplicable mystical experience.
Reformed: All who are justified will grow in sanctification. Of the major views presented here this is the only one that does not teach some form of crisis experience as necessary for sanctification. Growth in the Lord, while uneven, will continue throughout the lifetime of the one who has been truly regenerated. If, in time, there is no evidence of spiritual development in the professing believer, the most likely reason is that he was not truly born again.

As can be seen solid Christians may differ to some degree concerning how progressive sanctification takes place, but all would agree on the primary biblical means producing growth that we will cover over the next four chapters. Let's begin with prayer.

The Necessity of Prayer

Few would doubt the importance of prayer in the life of a believer and several passages of Scripture directly affirm prayer's role in our spiritual development. Hebrews 4:14–16, for example, informs us that "we do not have a great high priest (Christ) who cannot sympathize with our weaknesses, but One who has been tempted in all things as we are, yet without sin." In the Old Testament the High Priest of Israel served as mediator between the people and God. Only he could go into the presence of God in the Holy of Holies, and then only once per year on the Day of Atonement. There he would offer a blood sacrifice for the sins of the people. But even such sacrifices could not completely atone for sin because "it is impossible for the blood of bulls and goats to take away sins" (Hebrews 10:4). What the animal sacrifices could not do Christ did in His once-for-all sacrifice for our sins (Hebrews 10:9–18). As a result the door is now open for those cleansed by the blood of Christ to "draw near with confidence to the throne of grace" (Hebrews 4:16a). At such times we are assured that we will "receive mercy and find grace to help in time of need" (Hebrews 4:16b).

The Lord has determined that the means by which He meets our need(s) is prayer. For instance, if our need is to deal with anxiety we are told not only to cease being anxious, but "in everything by prayer and supplication with thanksgiving [to] let your requests be made known to God" (Philippians4:6), which will lead to the peace of God.

In the context of sickness, James points us to prayer, not just our own but that of others, particularly the elders of the church (James 5:13–18). The word for "sick" in James 5:14 is *astheneo* meaning "to be weak, feeble, to be without strength, powerless," according to *Strong's Concordance*. It is found 36 times in the New Testament, and its meaning is dependent upon the context. The word for "sick" in James 5:15 is a different word (*kamnonta*) which is found only two other times in the New Testament (Hebrews 12:3 and Revelation 2:3), where the meaning is clearly "weary." James does not seem to have in mind physical illness as much as spiritual and emotional weariness. When the child of God is facing times of spiritual exhaustion and weariness he or she should turn to prayer—not just personal, private prayer, but to the prayers of others as well. James 5:16 reads, "Therefore, confess your sins to one another, and pray for one another so that you may be healed. The effective prayer of a righteous man [which] can accomplish much." It is prayer that we need in such times.

First Timothy 2:1–2 calls God's people to pray for all people, particularly those in authority "so that we may lead a tranquil and quiet life in all godliness and dignity." Prayer is vital for living godly lives. In verse eight, corporate public prayer is in view when Paul writes, "Therefore I want the men in every place to pray, lifting up holy hands, without wrath and dissension." Again, both private and public prayers are important in true discipleship of individuals and the church.

Romans 8:26–29 is speaking in the direct context of discipleship, that is, being "conformed to the image of His Son" (v. 29). The text begins with a warning that "we do not know how to pray as we should," and therefore the Holy Spirit "helps our weakness ..., interceding for us with groanings too deep for words." Note carefully that we are not being told that the Holy Spirit speaks to us or gives us "groanings" that are equivalent to Him speaking through us. Rather He intercedes for us, that is, He is taking our prayers, as feeble and misplaced as they might sometimes be, and interceding on our behalf in such a way that the petition coming before the Father is in accordance with His will and purpose (vv. 27–28). These Spirit-interceded prayers are now used to conform those the Father has predestined, and called, and justified, and glorified, to the image of Jesus Christ (vv. 29–30). This is true spiritual formation or, better, transformation, and our prayers as translated by the Holy Spirit are at the center of such spiritual change.

We can be certain then that prayer is a God-ordained means by which the people of God are molded into His image. However, there is one more matter we need to concern ourselves with, especially in light of one of the key disciplines within the Spiritual Formation Movement—contemplative prayer. In a previous chapter contemplative prayer was defined as a form of praying in which the mind is by-passed. The goal of such praying is not cognitive, rational, or intellectual presentation of our petitions, confession or worship to God, but a mystical approach in an attempt to experience an inexplicable moment of ecstasy with God. Such ecstasy is supposed to lead us to a deep but incomprehensible union with the Lord. But is contemplative prayer the kind of prayer prescribed, modeled and taught in Scripture? Not at all. Let's take a look.

What is Biblical Prayer?

The Bible is filled with prayers. The book of Psalms alone, being the prayer and song book of Old Testament Israel, provides us with over 100 prayers which serve as models for our own prayer life. The prayers of hundreds of individuals are recorded for us in Scripture to study, examine, and be edified by. In addition we are given instructions on how to pray. The Scriptures do not leave us without adequate information on the subject of prayer. As a matter of fact, the most difficult task is to narrow down all that is written on and about prayer and select a few representative texts to enlighten our prayer lives. For this study we will choose just four such passages.

Matthew 6:9–13 is often called the Lord's Prayer. In the

middle of Jesus' best known sermon, "The Sermon on the Mount," He provides clear instructions to His disciples on how He wanted them to pray. At a later time, the disciples ask Jesus to teach them how to pray, and the Lord offers virtually the same guidelines (Luke 11:1–4). What is important for our purposes is to note that Jesus called for clear, intellectual praying that involved a person's cognitive thinking. We are to offer praise to God, urge the coming of His kingdom to earth, seek our daily needs, ask for forgiveness of sins, and pray for protection from temptation. There is no hint, in this greatest of instructional prayers, of extra-sensory experiences in which the mind is passive.

The prayers found in the epistles are wonderful models of biblical praying as well. As Paul prayed for the various churches we get an excellent understanding of what intercessory prayer looks like. Ephesians contains two of these prayers, the first in 1:15–23. Here we find Paul deeply desirous for the spiritual enhancement of the believers in this first century church. He wants their spiritual eyes opened so that they would "know of the hope of His calling, what are the riches of the glory of His inheritance in the saints and what is the surpassing greatness of His power toward us who believe" (1:18b-19a). All of this, Paul informs them, is "in accordance with the working of the strength of His might which he brought about in Christ ..." (1:19b-20a). He goes on to highlight the person and greatness of both the Father and the Son. Here is no mantra being repeated time and again leading to some form of intellectual and emotional purgation. Rather we hear firm and powerful requests that Paul continuously makes on the Ephesians' behalf (1:16).

Later in the same epistle the apostle adds some additional requests in a subsequent prayer (3:14–21). In this prayer he asks that these believers would be strengthened with power through the Holy Spirit, that Christ might dwell in their hearts by faith, that they might be rooted and grounded in love and comprehend all that the Lord has for them, including his surpassing love of Christ, leading to all the fullness of God. He closes with a great chorus of praise to the Lord Himself (3:20–21). Once again there is no ambiguity in this prayer. There is praise to God and petitions for the believers.

In Philippians 4:6–9, Paul teaches the first century believers (and us) how to pray, especially in the context of disharmony among believers (4:2–5) and the need for God's peace in life's circumstances (4:6). We are told to pray about everything and to do so with supplication. That is, we are to make our requests known to God (v. 6b). As a result we should experience God's peace, a peace beyond our comprehension. In each of these cases, and they could be multiplied many times over, the prayer originates from our minds. They are rational, intellectual prayers. But at the same time they are not devoid of emotion or experience.

One cannot read these prayers by Paul without recognizing
that they arise from the passionate heart of a man deeply
devoted to and in love with the Lord. But they are not
mindless prayers filled with techniques on how to have
subjective experiences. Nor are we taught to focus on our
breathing or to repeat over and over certain catch phrases
of mantras in order to center ourselves on God. We are
be taught to use our minds bringing real needs, concerns,
petitions and thanksgivings to the Lord. What we are seeing
is an important distinction between biblical praying and
practices taught in Scripture and contemplative praying
as practiced and taught by ancient monks, hermits and
promoters of the Spiritual Formation Movement today.
Prayer is absolutely essential for spiritual growth. But it must
be prayer that is taught and shaped by the Scriptures rather
than ancient and modern ideas and traditions of men.

10

Biblical Discipleship—
the Scriptures

When we speak of discipleship or Christian maturity, it must be understood from the beginning that all spiritual transformation is a supernatural work of God. Just as the natural man cannot will himself to be born again, so the Christian is dependent upon the Lord for inward change and growth. In Ephesians 3:16–17 Paul prays for the Ephesian believers "that He would grant you, according to the riches of His glory, to be strengthened with power through His Spirit in the inner man, so that Christ may dwell in your hearts through faith ..." But before

He strengthens us with power the Lord must give us new life. This new life is the result of a spiritual birth, being born again (or from above) (John 3:3), or regeneration. Titus 3:5 reads, "He saved us, not on the basis of deeds which we have done in righteousness, but according to His mercy, by the washing of regeneration and renewing by the Holy Spirit ..." Just as our regeneration is a supernatural work of God, so is our progressive sanctification. But the Holy Spirit does not work in a vacuum; He uses means to bring about our spiritual development and the primary means, the one most spoken of in Scripture, is the Word of God.

Romans 12:2 tells us we are transformed by the renewing of our minds. Our thinking does not change unless there is new information for our minds to process. In my college days a rumor was floating around among some of the students that if you slept with your head on your text book or notes, your brain would absorb the necessary knowledge for the next day's exam. Against my better judgment I gave this method a try once and concluded via the next day's exam that this technique does not work. Similarly, spiritual transformation does not take place by osmosis. Apart from a renewing of our minds by means of the input of the truth of God's Word we will not be changed. We need to take a close look at what role Scripture claims for itself in the spiritual transformation process.

Scriptures Claim to Have Transformative Powers

In our Lord's great prayer on the night He was betrayed, as found in John 17, His thoughts were focused on His disciples. As Jesus contemplates the great struggles they will have in a world that hates them and from a devil who wants to destroy them, He asked the Father to sanctify them (John 17:17a). To sanctify is to set someone or something apart. As stated earlier when used in the New Testament, in the context of the Christian life, the meaning is to set apart for a holy purpose. Jesus prays that His disciples are kept separated from the polluting influences of the world around them so that they might live as the Lord intended and fulfill the mission they would be given of making disciples. Jesus goes on to clarify how they are to be sanctified when He prays, "Sanctify them in truth; Your word is truth" (v. 17b). The battle the disciples would wage would be largely in the realm of truth. If they are compromised by a worldview dominated by sinful impulses and demonic insight, they will be unfruitful in making disciples for Christ. In order to be effective in their discipleship endeavors it will be necessary for them to be saturated with truth. And Jesus makes clear that the truth He speaks of does not emerge from the culture or the wisdom of humans but from God's Word. Their great weapon in this fight against the darkness of sin and spiritual blindness will be the "sword of the Spirit, which is the word of God" (Ephesians 6:17). Later, when Paul addresses the early church on the process of change and growth, he tells them to "lay aside the old self" and "put on the new self" and "be renewed by the spirit of your mind" (Ephesians 4:22–24). The renewing of our mind—the way we think, the way we process what enters our minds, the way we approach life itself, must be changed through the truth, which is found in the Word of God.

As we contemplate Scripture's place in our spiritual development we must return for a moment to the foundational role of the Lord Himself. The third chapter in Second Corinthians speaks of the hardening of the minds of the Old Testament Jews (v. 14a). Even as Paul pens his inspired epistle he says it is like they have a veil over their minds and hearts (vv. 14b, 15) that disabled the first century Jews from seeing who Christ really was. But when a person turns to Christ that veil is removed (v. 16). The believer can now see what they could not in their unregenerate state—the glory of the Lord. Paul writes, "But we all with unveiled face, beholding as in a mirror the glory of the Lord, are being transformed into the same image from glory to glory, just as from the Lord, the Spirit" (v. 18). To be sure, the unbeliever can read and understand the details of Scripture. Even some scholarly and mostly accurate commentaries on the Bible have been written by non-Christians. But the unregenerate cannot comprehend the true glory of Christ, or know Him as Savior and Lord, until the spiritual veil has been removed at the moment of conversion. The unbeliever cannot grasp the gospel both because he does not have the spiritual capacity to do so, and because Satan has blinded him to the glory of

Christ. Paul continues, "And even if our gospel is veiled, it is veiled to those who are perishing, in whose case the god of this world has blinded the minds of the unbelievers so that they might not see the light of the gospel of the glory of Christ, who is the image of God" (4:3–4). Those who are perishing (present tense—not will perish, but are already doing so) can understand the details of Christology and soteriology, but they cannot grasp the significance of the gospel because it reveals the glory of Christ which they cannot truly see.

Due to this spiritual blindness the unbeliever is in a hopeless bind. He is blind, cannot comprehend Christ's true nature and glory, and is in bondage to Satan—the god of this age. To add to their woes Paul tells us in Ephesians 2:1–3 that the unsaved are dead in their trespasses and sins, merely following the course of the world, are children of disobedience, enslaved to their own lusts and under the wrath of God. Our situation is indeed hopeless, "But God, being rich in mercy, because of His great love with which He loved us … made us alive together with Christ …" (Ephesians 2:4–5). Through a supernatural work of God we have been born again—given spiritual life. In 2 Corinthians 4:6 Paul describes this spiritual transaction this way, "For God, who said, 'Light shall shine out of darkness,' is the One who has shone in our hearts to give the Light of the knowledge of the glory of God in the face of Christ." The very God who in the act of creation separated light from darkness, is the same God who turns on the spiritual light in our hearts so we might be able to comprehend the glory of Himself as found in His Son.

These biblical texts reveal the supernatural nature and requirement of regeneration. We cannot give ourselves new life; it is a gift from God. As Jesus said, salvation is not hard, it is impossible—apart from the intervention of God (Mark 10:27). This brings us back to the subject at hand. Now that the Lord God has removed our spiritual veil, has revealed His glory through His Son and given us new life in Him, we are in the position to be progressively transformed by the power of the Spirit through the means God supplies. In 2 Corinthians 3:18, the believer is privileged to "behold as in a mirror the glory of the Lord." Ancient mirrors were usually made of polished metals and, unlike modern mirrors, they would lack the near perfect reflection we enjoy today. This picture communicated to the original readers that while they could now view the image of Christ it would not be with absolute perfection and clarity which remains for a future time (see 1 Corinthians 13:12 and 1 John 3:2). Nevertheless, we are promised that as we "behold … the glory of the Lord" we are being transformed into Christ's image. This promise reminds us of Romans 8:28–29 that speaks of us being called, foreknown, and predestined "to become conformed to the image of His Son." A marvelous part of God's redemption plan is the believer's conformity to Christ-likeness. Our Lord is not content with saving us and leaving us virtually unchanged. Rather as Christians "we are His workmanship, created in Christ Jesus for good works, which God prepared beforehand so that we would walk in them" (Ephesians 2:10).

All of this begs the question—what means does the Holy Spirit ordain to conform us to Christ's image? If we are being transformed into His image as we behold His glory, as promised in 2 Corinthians 3:18, just how do we go about beholding His glory? Since we do not see Him physically today how are we to see His glory so that we can be transformed? I believe God has chosen Scripture to play the role of revealing Christ's glory to His people. Many biblical passages detail the transformational nature of the inspired text of Scripture. Our Father has chosen to use His written Word, combined with the power of His Spirit, to change us and enable us to grow toward conformity with His Son. Let's take a closer look.

Old Testament Teachings

The New Testament unmistakably supports the above thesis, but the Old Testament is on the same page, as we might expect. Deuteronomy 29:29, for example, states, "The secret things belong to the Lord our God, but the things revealed belong to us and to our sons forever, that we may observe all the work of this Law." Much like today, the people of Moses' time apparently wanted to be privy to the secret counsels and will of God. Not content with what God had revealed to them, they wanted knowledge of the future and insight into God's sovereign plans and the reasons behind His actions.

Moses makes it clear that some things are for God alone and we are not invited to His inner councils. However, the Lord has revealed many things to His people. These things, recorded by men but inspired by God, are ours forever. By this means we are able to observe His will and live accordingly.

Another favorite from the Old Testament is Psalm 19. The first six verses deal with God's revelation through nature. The physical universe reveals certain things about God such as His glory and creative powers. Romans 1:18–20 adds that the Lord's invisible attributes, eternal power and divine nature are clearly seen in that which He has created—so that rebellious mankind is without excuse when it rejects Him. But what we learn of God through creation has limits. The general power, nature, and glory of God are evident, but many details are missing. No one could ever discern a great number of truths about God by gazing at the stars or hiking through the rain forest or sailing the seas. We would never understand Christ, sin, salvation, the necessity of the cross, the resurrection and much more, for such things need specific revelation from our Creator. In verse seven of Psalm 19, David turns from general revelation, as found in observation of the universe around us, to specific revelation, the written Word of God. He speaks of the Law in particular as perfect, sure, right, pure, clean, true, desirable, sweet, and providing warning for those who disobey the commandments of God. They will be restored, made wise, rejoice, be enlightened, and rewarded (vv. 7–14). The Psalmist can't seem to find enough wonderful things to say about

God's Word, but Psalm 19 pales in comparison to Psalm 119. One hundred and seventy three verses out of 176 speak of the grandeur and/or power and profitability of the written Word. Just a sampling sees why the Psalmist is so excited: It is by treasuring the Lord's Word in one's heart that we are kept from sin (v. 11). We can keep our way pure by living according to God's Word (v. 9). Affliction is explained by the Word as coming from the hand of a faithful God and is good for us (vv. 67, 71, 75, 92). The Lord's Word cannot be changed (v. 89), and much more.

The Old Testament is very clear about the role Scripture plays in enabling God's people to change, grow, and live according to the Lord's glory. But the New Testament is even clearer.

New Testament Teachings

The New Testament claims that the Scriptures contribute a number of spiritual benefits. For example:

Salvation

Especially in light of reported claims today of people coming to Christ through dreams, visions, and unusual experiences of all kinds, it is important to note Scripture's role in our salvation. Romans 10:17 tells us that "faith comes from hearing, and hearing by the word of Christ." People simply cannot come to a saving knowledge of Christ without input from the Word of Christ. It is the Scripture that reveals the absolute holiness of God, that enables us to see our sinfulness and need for salvation, that describes and explains the Lord's redemption plan through Christ's sacrifice on the cross and resurrection, which informs us that salvation cannot be obtained by our good works and that we receive the gift of eternal life through faith alone. There is no way that any of us could know the content of the gospel apart from the divine revelation found in the Bible. As Paul trains Timothy in his faith and ministries, he encourages the younger man to continue in the things that Paul had taught him (2 Timothy 3:14). Of first importance is that from childhood Timothy has known the "sacred writings ... able to give you wisdom that leads to salvation through faith which is in Christ Jesus" (3:15). Paul's concern was that Timothy not detach himself from the things Paul had taught him, including the part Scripture plays in salvation, and substitute some of the new theological trends beginning to manifest themselves in the early days of Christianity (2:14–26). Timothy must be totally convinced of the necessity of the sacred writings to bring people to Christ.

In 1 Corinthians, Paul refers to the gospel message as the "word of the cross." He warns that to "those who are perishing the cross is foolishness" but "to us who are being saved it is the power of God" (1:18). This statement is immediately reinforced by quoting Isaiah 29:14 from the Old Testament (1:19). Similarly, Romans 1:16–17 speaks of the gospel as "the power of God for salvation to everyone who believes." Again Paul's claims for the gospel are backed by

Scripture, "As it is written, 'but the righteous man shall live by faith'" (1:17b). The place of Scripture is pivotal in our salvation. It in fact reveals the power of God for salvation. Without Scripture we would neither know the work of the cross nor be able to apply it to our lives. No one is saved apart from the application of the gospel which is found only in the Bible.

Transformative Powers

Romans 12:2 has already been referenced, and is perhaps the key text explaining the role of Scripture in our sanctification, but it is certainly not alone. If transformation takes place through the renewing of our minds as Romans 12:2 claims, then renewing of our minds comes about through the knowledge of the Word as the Old Testament has already affirmed. But several New Testament passages echo this same thought. In Acts chapter twenty, we find Paul instructing the Ephesian elders concerning guarding and instructing the church in his absence: "Now I commend you to God and to the Word of His grace, which is able to build you up and to give you the inheritance among all those who are sanctified" (v. 32). If the saints are to be "built up" then the elders must be diligent to teach the Word of grace. It was through this means that the saints would grow.

Peter's inspired writings are in agreement. In 1 Peter 2:2 he urges the believers to be "like newborn babies, long[ing] for the pure milk of the word, so that by it you may grow in respect to salvation." If the children of God are to grow up they must imitate babies who grow because they receive nourishment. Many Christians wonder why they have never grown much in their spiritual lives, but upon closer examination these believers often have fed very little on the Word. No one would be surprised to learn that an undernourished child does not grow and develop properly. The same principle applies spiritually. Growth is dependent upon wholesome intake of the Word of God.

In Peter's second epistle he adds that Christ's "divine power has granted to us everything pertaining to life and godliness, through the true knowledge of Him who called us by His own glory and excellence" (1:3). The word "everything" leaves no room for competing input. If spiritual life and godliness is to be attained, the sole means is through the true knowledge of Christ, which can only be attained through the Scriptures. But what about those who elevate experience above God's revelation, or others who view dreams and mystical encounters as being superior? Peter is ready for such claims. In the same chapter he recalls a real-life experience, as opposed to a mystical one, in which he and others witnessed the glory of the Lord at the Transfiguration (1:16–18). Still, Peter writes, there was something better than that—the Scriptures themselves (1:19–21). No prophet, he declares, made up his prophecy but rather was inspired by the Holy Spirit. In his understanding of Christ, Peter is saying, Scripture trumps even real experiences. Experiences are subjective and can be misunderstood or even altered in our minds over time.

Memories are not static and are therefore unreliable. Not so the objective inspired Scriptures.

Hebrews 4:12 informs us that "the Word of God is living and active, sharper than any two-edged sword, piercing to the division of soul and spirit, of joints and of marrow, and discerning the thoughts and intentions of the heart." The Scriptures reveal our hearts and thoughts which is necessary for dealing with sin and walking in the path of righteousness. This verse is the perfect follow-up to David's prayer in Psalm 139:23–24, "Search me, O God, and know my heart; try me and know my anxious thoughts; and see if there be any hurtful way in me, and lead me in the everlasting way." Wonderful prayer, but how was David expecting God to reveal these matters to him and in turn lead him in the right direction? Hebrews 4:12 answers these questions. The Lord exposes the heart and leads through His revealed Scriptures. James 1:21–25 warns however that the Word behaves as a mirror revealing our spiritual blemishes. When this happens we can either deal with what the Word discloses or we can walk away and ignore what we have seen. It is the "effective doer," not the "forgetful hearer," James says, who will be blessed in what he does (v. 25).

This brings us back to the important writings of Paul. We turn first to the book of Ephesians. In 4:11–16, Paul is outlining how the church of Christ functions. Gifted men have been given to the church (v. 11) for the task of equipping the saints to minister and building up the body of Christ (v. 12). Maturity is the goal (vv. 13–14), so that believers are able to speak the truth in love enabling fellow believers to "grow up in all aspects into Him who is the head, even Christ" (v. 15). When this takes place the whole body functions as it was intended resulting in "growth of the body for the building up of itself in love" (v. 16). What a beautiful picture all hinging on the gifted men of verse eleven fulfilling their God-ordained role of equipping the saints "for the work of service" (v. 12). The issue at hand is how are the gifted men to equip the saints? To help us get a handle on this, we need to understand what the word "equip" means. The word was used in New Testament times for resetting of broken bones and mending of ripped nets. What the doctor did for his patients with broken arms, and what the fisherman did with his broken nets, so the gifted men are to do for the saints. Broken bones and ripped nets need to be mended or else they will never serve their purposes as they were designed to do. The gifted men equip or mend broken and torn up lives. As people come to Christ, they come with lives wreaked by sin and in need of repair. The gifted men have been assigned the task of mending these lives. The next question is how do the gifted men mend ("equip") these broken saints? There could be many guesses but guessing is unnecessary—Paul supplied the answer in 2 Timothy 3:16–17. In one of the greatest treatises on Scripture in the Word of God, Paul is explaining that the Bible, which is God-breathed, is profitable for four things: to teach us about God, ourselves and how we are to live; to reprove us, pointing out our sin; to correct us, showing us how to overcome sin; and to train us, so that we can walk in the path of righteousness. When all this takes place Paul assures us that "we will be adequate, equipped for every good work" (v. 17). Here we run into our word "equip" again. What is it that equips us for every good work? Paul is clear—it is the proper use of the Word of God. The gifted men mend broken lives and enable the body to function as designed by equipping the saints through the diligent teaching of the Word of God. It is no wonder that Paul immediately charges Timothy to preach the Word (2 Timothy 4:1–5), for only through the proclamation of the Word will the children of God be equipped for every good work.

It should be recalled that Paul does not give these instructions to Timothy without a context. The whole epistle of 2 Timothy has been leading up to this. In 2 Timothy 2:2 Paul has commissioned Timothy to take the truths that Paul has given him (which Paul had received from Christ) and pass them on to faithful men who would do the same with other faithful men. But Timothy could not do this if he himself was not "diligent to present [him]self-approved to God as a workman who does not need to be ashamed, accurately handling the word of truth" (2:15). If Timothy was to pass on to others the word of truth he had to study it in order to accurately proclaim it. Equipping saints is hard work and to do it well requires diligent study, so that the word of truth is handled accurately, or "cut straight" as a literal translation of this verse might read.

As we have seen, the use of the Scriptures as the means of spiritual transformation is not an incidental matter. Scripture proclaims itself to be at the very heart of any change and all growth in the life of the saint. Conformity to the image of Christ is not possible without the Holy Spirit applying the Word of God. But it is one thing to strongly believe in the power of the Word, it is another to accurately apply it to our lives. We need to turn next to application.

Application

By way of application, I want to emphasize four things:

Proper Interpretation

The importance of accurately handling the Word has already been mentioned (2 Timothy 2:15) but we need to return to this briefly. There are many Christians who strongly proclaim their love for the Bible and yet seldom open it. Others may read a verse or two per day but do not meditate on what they read. And even those who dedicate themselves to a regiment of study may misinterpret, and thus misapply, what they read. When we are told to accurately handle, or cut straight, the Word of truth, this presupposes that such is possible. While some texts and themes are difficult to understand, and are subject to disagreement even among sound believers, the majority of Scripture is clear with even a small amount of study and effort. The real cause of most confusion and disagreement is not the plain teaching found in a passage but the hermeneutical approach being used. Hermeneutics is the science and art of interpretation. We use hermeneutics every time we read anything—from the newspapers to a novel to our tax forms. Most often we interpret what we read literally, or normally. When it comes to the Bible this is often called a historical-grammatical approach, simply meaning that we interpret the Bible according to the rules of grammar and in its historical context. As I have said, this is how we interpret virtually everything we read. But strangely when it comes to Scripture numerous other interpretative theories have been invented. Some of the more complicated ones include neo-orthodoxy and redemptive-spirit hermeneutics. But for the average student of Scripture it is the allegorical and devotional methods that cause most of the damage. These approaches seek hidden and secondary meaning behind the obvious. When applied to a biblical text, the intended meaning is brushed aside and replaced with an imaginative meaning which goes beyond the clear teaching of the passage. Through these methods Scripture can be twisted to mean anything the reader wants it to mean and in the process God's communication to us is marred and mutilated. The world of Paul and Timothy was no stranger to allegoricalism, this having become common prior to the church age. It is for this reason that Paul demands that Timothy work hard at accurately interpreting the Word. The lazy can and will pervert the teaching of God's Word, the serious Christian must be careful not to do so. When we do not interpret Scripture in a normal fashion, as it was meant to be read, we will mute its marvelous message and be the poorer for it.

Growth in Discernment

The author of Hebrews, in chapter five, wants to explain to his readers how Jesus is now their high priest after the order of Melchizedek. Sadly, the author fears they will not understand this valuable teaching because they have become "dull of hearing" (v. 11), and this because they have not matured in their understanding of spiritual things and now are in need of being taught again the "elementary principles of the oracles of God" (vv. 12–13). He reminded his readers that solid spiritual food is only for the mature (v. 14a). And how does one gain such maturity? By training their senses to discern good and evil (v. 14b). We find here no sympathy for baby Christians who have been saved for many years but have not grown in their understanding of the deeper things of God. Rather because they have stayed stagnant in their spiritual development they are missing out on valuable understanding of the person and work of Jesus Christ.

Inward Dwelling

Paul admonishes the Colossians to "let the word of Christ richly dwell within" them (Colossians 3:16). To richly dwell means to be at home within them. As Christians the Colossians were indwelt by Christ through the agency of the Holy Spirit (1 Corinthians 6:19), but here Paul desires that Christ's very words find a home in their hearts. Home is where we feel comfortable and accepted. Christ's word should receive that same kind of reception with us. When it does, we will find ourselves teaching with wisdom, exhorting one another, experiencing thankfulness and living out our lives in the name of the Lord (3:16b–17).

Exhorting and Refuting in Sound Doctrine

When the Word of Christ is richly dwelling in us it should be natural that we want to share God's truth with others. As Paul lays out requirements for elders in his letter to Titus, he first details personal, godly qualities and then turns to one related to the Word. An elder is to hold "fast the faithful word which is in accordance with the teaching, so that he will be able to exhort in sound doctrine and to refute those who contradict" [sound doctrine] (Titus 1:9). Elders must hold fast, clinging to the Word of God. They must have a tenacious desire to not be moved from its truth. But more than that, they must know the Word well enough that they can exhort or encourage others in the faith, in the sound doctrine or teaching of the Word. And even further, when necessary they will be able to show the error of those who teach false doctrine. This assumes that an elder has carefully studied Scripture and theology to the point that he can take both positive and negative stands for truth as he leads and protects the local church.

Similarly Paul calls for Timothy to retain and guard the

sound words of Scripture (2 Timothy 1:13–14). Timothy was not to seek new revelation nor adopt the philosophies, imaginations and speculations of those around him. He was to "retain [maintain, cling to] the standard of sound words which you have heard from me [Paul]." As the inspired writer of Scripture and apostle of Christ, Paul had been given the "sound words" of the faith. He handed these down to many others including Timothy. Timothy was to retain and guard these sound words as well as "entrust these to faithful men who will be able to teach others also" (2 Timothy 2:2). The servants of Christ are not to be creative in what they teach. They are to take the sound word first given to the human authors of Scripture by the Holy Spirit (2 Timothy 3:16), and hand them down to faithful believers who will do likewise.

This important treasure of sound words will surely be subject to attack by demonic forces and evil men. So Timothy is to also "guard, through the Holy Spirit who dwells in us, the treasure which has been entrusted to you" (2 Timothy 1:14). Jude appeals to his readers to "contend earnestly for the faith which was once for all handed down to the saints. For certain persons have crept in unnoticed … ungodly persons who turn the grace of our God into licentiousness and deny our only Master and Lord, Jesus Christ" (vv. 3–4). If "the faith," which is synonymous with the doctrines of the faith, is so precious and valuable and such a treasure, it is only natural that those who love it will fight for it.

Conclusion

The result of a biblically informed use of Scripture is spiritual growth. Second Peter 1:3–8 states:

> Seeing that His divine power has granted to us everything pertaining to life and godliness, through the true knowledge of Him who called us by His own glory and excellence. For by these He has granted to us His precious and magnificent promises, so that by them you may become partakers of *the* divine nature, having escaped the corruption that is in the world by lust. Now for this very reason also, applying all diligence, in your faith supply moral excellence, and in *your* moral excellence, knowledge, and in *your* knowledge, self-control, and in *your* self-control, perseverance, and in *your* perseverance, godliness, and in *your* godliness, brotherly kindness and in *your* brotherly kindness, love. For if these *qualities* are yours and are increasing, they render you neither useless nor unfruitful in the true knowledge of our Lord Jesus Christ.

No wonder John wrote, "I have no greater joy than this, to hear of my children walking in the truth" (3 John 4).

As we consider the means by which spiritual change, growth and development takes place we find that the Scriptures constantly point the believer to the very inspired words it contains. We need not look to extra-biblical sources such as those found in the Spiritual Formation Movement, among others. Growth in godliness comes primarily through the power of the Holy Spirit who enables believers to understand and apply the Word of God to their lives.

11

Biblical Discipleship— Fellowship

A s we continue to pursue the specific means found in Scripture that the Lord has given us to aid in spiritual growth, we now turn to the subject of fellowship. We are reminded at this point that some within the Spiritual Formation Movement claim that virtually anything can become a means of spiritual formation. But without specific biblical support it is presumptuous on our part to infuse some activity, no matter how spiritual or pious it may seem, with qualities which aid our progressive sanctification. If we are to be true to the inspired text of

Scripture we must search for instruments which the Holy Spirit has explicitly proclaimed to be means of promoting discipleship. So far we have found that both biblical prayer and the Scriptures are two such activities. Now we will examine another, that of fellowship with other believers, and the body of Christ.

Fellowship—What Is It?

One of the Greek words that the average Christian is likely to know is *koinonia*. The word is found 19 times in the New Testament and means fellowship, communion, participation, or sharing. William Mounce writes, "This mutual sharing is seen in the description of the newly founded church in Acts 2:42, in which one of the four patterns of discipleship is the early Christians' continuing together in *koinonia*."[262] Fellowship of believers has been an important means of making disciples since the establishment of the church.

Perhaps the central passage on this subject is Hebrews 10:24–25. The epistle to the Hebrews was written to an unknown group of mostly Jewish believers who seemed to be retreating in their spiritual walk. Most believe that this was a second or third generation of Christians that had perhaps lost the wonder of their salvation and the joys of what they possessed in Christ, and were being enticed back to Old Testament Jewish rituals and, to some degree, doctrines. They did not seem to realize that many of these Old Covenant structures, such as the priesthood, and many practices, such as the sacrifices, were mere shadows of better things to come (see 10:1). Having lost their interest in the realities found in Christ and the superior ways of worshiping the Lord on this side of the cross, the Hebrew believers were not only drifting back toward Judaism but had seemingly lost their enthusiasm for fellowship with one another. The inspired author of Hebrews was concerned for both their doctrine and practices when he wrote,

> Let us hold fast the confession of our hope without wavering, for He who promised is faithful; and let us consider how to stimulate one another to love and good deeds, not forsaking our own assembling together, as is the habit of some, but encouraging one another; and all the more as you see the day drawing near (10:23–25).

Rather than forsaking the assembly and living out their individual lives, they were to consider how they could stimulate fellow believers to love one another and to do good things for Christ. In addition they should be an encouragement to one another as they met together for worship, study of the Word and fellowship. Rather than being individualistic and self-focused, they were to be Christ-centered and concerned for the well-being and needs of others in the church and unbelievers on the outside.

We have all, on occasion, dialogued with people who declare themselves to be Christians but are not involved in a local church. For one reason or another they will claim they have no need for the body of Christ, as they are perfectly content to live out their Christian experience apart from other believers. When I run into such people I challenge them to consider not just themselves but others as well. Even if a true believer could live flawlessly without other Christians, something I would deny is possible based upon the New Testament, such a mature believer should consider how valuable they would be in helping weaker saints in their spiritual journeys. It is interesting that the author of Hebrews does not attempt to motivate his audience to assemble because it was good for them personally but in order to find ways of helping others. If anyone could be a spiritual island unto himself, it would surely have been an apostle, and yet the driving passion of all the apostles was to make disciples as Jesus had commanded (Matthew 28:19–20). When Paul penned his last inspired epistle to his child in the faith Timothy, he simply re-worded Jesus' Great Commission:

> The things which you have heard from me in the presence of many witnesses, entrust these to faithful men who will be able to teach others also (2 Timothy 2:2).

It is impossible to entrust faithful people with the Word of God, i.e. make disciples, and not meet with them on a regular basis. If the primary task of disciples is to make disciples, as Jesus mandated, then personal involvement of believers with one another is absolutely necessary.

One Another

The essence and importance of Christian fellowship is nowhere more clearly emphasized than in the repetition of the term "one another" as found in the New Testament. Below are 59 references in which the disciple of Christ is told to do something for "one another." It is both instructive and impressive to see these listed:

1. "Be at peace with one another" (Mark 9:50)

2. "Wash one another's feet" (John 13:14)

3. "Love one another" (John 13:34)

4. "Love one another" (John 13:34)

5. "Love one another" (John 13:35)

6. "Love one another" (John 15:12)

7. "Love one another" (John 15:17)

8. "Be devoted to one another in brotherly love" (Romans 12:10)

9. "Honor one another above yourselves" (Romans 12:10)

10. "Live in harmony with one another" (Romans 12:16)

11. "Love one another" (Romans 13:8)

12. "Stop passing judgment on one another" (Romans 14:13)

13. "Accept one another, then, just as Christ accepted you" (Romans 15:7)

14. "Instruct one another" (Romans 15:14)

15. "Greet one another with a holy kiss" (Romans 16:16)

16. "When you come together to eat, wait for one another" (1 Cor. 11:33)

17. "Have equal concern for each other" (1 Corinthians 12:25)

18. "Greet one another with a holy kiss" (1 Corinthians 16:20)

19. "Greet one another with a holy kiss" (2 Corinthians 13:12)

20. "Serve one another in love" (Galatians 5:13)

21. "If you keep on biting and devouring each other ... you will be destroyed by one another" (Galatians 5:15)

22. "Let us not become conceited, provoking and envying one another" (Galatians 5:26)

23. "Carry one another's burdens" (Galatians 6:2)

24. "Be patient, bearing with one another in love" (Ephesians 4:2)

25. "Be kind and compassionate to one another" (Ephesians 4:32)

26. "Forgiving each other" (Ephesians 4:32)

27. "Speak to one another with psalms, hymns and spiritual songs" (Ephesians 5:19)

28. "Submit to one another out of reverence for Christ" (Ephesians 5:21)

29. "In humility consider others better than yourselves" (Philippians 2:3)

30. "Do not lie to each other" (Colossians 3:9)

31. "Bear with each other" (Colossians 3:13)

32. "Forgive whatever grievances you may have against one another" (Colossians 3:13)

33. "Teach [one another]" (Colossians 3:16)

34. "Admonish one another (Colossians 3:16)

35. "Make your love increase and overflow for each other" (1 Thessalonians 3:12)

36. "Love each other" (1 Thessalonians 4:9)

37. "Comfort one another" (1 Thessalonians 4:18)

38. "Encourage each other" (1 Thessalonians 5:11)

39. "Build each other up" (1 Thessalonians 5:11)

40. "Encourage one another daily" Hebrews 3:13)

41. "Spur one another on toward love and good deeds" (Hebrews 10:24)

42. "Encourage one another" (Hebrews 10:25)

43. "Do not slander one another" (James 4:11)

44. "Don't grumble against one another" (James 5:9)

45. "Confess your sins to one another" (James 5:16)

46. "Pray for one another" (James 5:16)

47. "Love one another deeply, from the heart" (1 Peter 3:8)

48. "Live in harmony with one another" (1 Peter 3:8)

49. "Love each other deeply" (1 Peter 4:8)

50. "Offer hospitality to one another without grumbling" (1 Peter 4:9)

51. "Each one should use whatever gift he has received to serve others" (1 Peter 4:10)

52. "Clothe yourselves with humility toward one another" (1 Peter 5:5)

53. "Greet one another with a kiss of love" (1 Peter 5:14)

54. "Love one another" (1 John 3:11)

55. "Love one another" (1 John 3:23)

56. "Love one another" (1 John 4:7)

57. "Love one another" (1 John 4:11)

58. "Love one another" (1 John 4:12)

59. "Love one another" (2 John 5)[263]

As with most lists, simply reading this one can almost lull one to sleep and if so we miss the importance of what is being said. Each of these commands should be read in context for its full impact. But even a quick glance at this extensive list reveals that some themes are repeated often, such as greeting one another, serving one another, forgiving one another and encouraging one another. But let us not miss that 21 Times we are told to love one another. In one form or other almost all of these "one another" commands are linked to love. And it is virtually impossible to demonstrate love to people with whom you have no involvement.

Of course the word love is often overused and abused in our society. We declare love for everything from chocolate to scenery to our spouse and children. To complicate matters our culture has a hard time defining love. If you were to ask the average person on Main Street how they knew that their spouse or family member loved them, they most likely would not give a biblical description. Fortunately when the Lord wanted to give us a look at real love He did two things. First, He showed us the example of Himself, especially through Christ. Jesus' life was and is a living illustration of what love looks like in human flesh. As He said in Mark 10:45, "For even the Son of Man did not come to be served, but to serve, and to give His life a ransom for many." And of course the cross is the ultimate example of self-sacrificing love. It was for this reason, when Paul is demanding that husbands love their wives, he said to do so "just as Christ also loved the church and gave Himself up for her" (Ephesians 5:25).

In addition to the example of perfect love, most fully demonstrated and realized in Christ, the Lord gave us not a mere definition but a full-orbed description of love. In 1 Corinthians 13 we are given 15 descriptions of what love is.

Love is patient, love is kind and is not jealous; love does not brag and is not arrogant, does not act unbecomingly; it does not seek its own, is not provoked, does not take into account a wrong suffered, does not rejoice in unrighteousness, but rejoices with the truth; bears all things, believes all things, hopes all things, endures all things. Love never fails.

In the Greek these are all verbs describing what love does. So the Lord is describing not so much feelings or abstracts but actions. This does not mean that love is devoid of emotion and affection (it certainly is not), but love is not to be reduced to sentimentalism. Looking closer we find the first two descriptions are positive, telling us what love is, while the next eight are negative, telling us what love is not. Then the last five move back to the positive. It is not my intention at this point to analyze these descriptions of love. But what I would have the reader note, both concerning the list of "one anothers" and this description of love, is that they are both completely focused on others. While this is obvious on the surface, it is not apparently so obvious to many Christians in everyday life. For example, ask most believers why they attend a certain church and the answer you will probably receive will have to do with the benefits they are receiving: the teaching is good, the music excels, the church has a good children and youth ministry, and so forth. You are less likely to hear that someone is involved in a local church because he or she can best serve the Lord there, yet serving others is the focus of love.

Conversely, ask a maverick believer why he does not attend church and you will likely hear that he gets nothing out of it or doesn't need to attend church to worship God, or the church is full of hypocrites and the like. Yet the emphasis in the New Testament is for the children of God to be part of the local church in order to give rather than receive. This is not to ignore texts such as Acts 2:42 in which the members of the first New Testament church came together to devote "themselves to the apostles' teaching and to fellowship, to the breaking of bread and to prayer." Foremost in the reasons given for gathering together was to receive the apostles' teaching, which is the body of New Testament truth as eventually written in the epistles. It is vital that we become part of a local assembly that clearly and systematically teaches sound doctrine and glorifies Christ. A gathering of Christians that does not devote themselves to the careful study of God's Word is not a biblical church by the standards of Scripture. But having found such a church, the followers of Christ should make it their passion to become the best lovers and servers of those around them that they can possibly be.

Greatness

The tendency of our flesh is to be self-centered, to be concerned for our own welfare instead of others, and to elevate self. The apostles exhibited these traits at numerous junctures right in the presence of their Lord. As a matter of fact, on three occasions, as revealed in the Gospels at the very points in which Jesus had just informed them of His impending redemptive work, we find that they either ignored or misunderstood Jesus' message. Each time Jesus not only rebuked them but also took the opportunity to teach them valuable lessons concerning discipleship, greatness and leadership:

True Discipleship: In Mark 8:31, for the first time Jesus clearly stated to His disciples that He would suffer, be rejected, be killed and would then return from the dead. The response by Peter, who seemed to represent the others, was a stern rebuke, after all, Peter reasoned, Jesus was headed to the seat of David, not a tomb (v. 32). Jesus cuts Peter short and rebukes him saying, "Get behind Me, Satan; for you are not setting your mind on God's interests, but man's" (v. 33). At this point Jesus launches into one of the most powerful and clear descriptions of what it means to be a true follower of His: "If anyone wishes to come after Me, he must deny himself, and take up his cross and follow Me. For whoever wishes to save his life will lose it, but whoever loses his life for My sake and the gospel's will save it" (vv. 34–35). Jesus has certainly set the bar high for the apostles and for all of us who claim to be His disciples. Our natural tendency is to be wrapped up in that little bundle called "us." The apostles certainly exhibit this trait and most of us fare no better. Yet Jesus calls us to deny ourselves—to remove our "selves" from the center of our lives. We are to then take up His cross. The cross symbolized death. Someone carrying a cross would have no need for personal agendas or ambitions. So too, the disciples of Christ should focus on doing the Master's will. And that would include following Him. True discipleship would depict a life lived for the will of the Savior, doing His work His way rather than living self-centeredly as is our natural bent.

True Greatness: The next time Jesus approached the subject of His death (Mark 9:31), the disciples did not understand what He was talking about and were afraid to ask (v. 32). In the meanwhile, as they walked from city to city eventually ending up in Capernaum, Jesus questioned their conversation along the way (v. 33), knowing that they had been discussing which one of them was the greatest (v. 34). Jesus pointedly said to them, "If anyone wants to be first, he shall be last of all and servant of all." He followed this statement with an objective lesson of taking a child in His arms and stating, "Whoever receives one child like this in My name receives Me …" (vv. 35–37). True greatness is not marked by being recognized as the best or the most powerful, but by humbly ministering to even the lowliest, most needy and helpless of people. The great in the world's eyes deal with dignitaries and make decisions that affect large numbers of people. Those who are great in God's eyes serve others in a spirit of meekness.

True Leadership: Not long afterward Jesus, for a third time, gave details to the apostles concerning His pending death and resurrection (Mark 10:33–34). Shortly thereafter James and John, who seemed to have dismissed Jesus' message without much consideration, asked if they could, in the kingdom, be given the prominent positions of power and authority (vv. 35–37). Jesus took the opportunity to define for them what true leadership looks like from God's perspective:

> You know that those who are recognized as rulers of the Gentiles lord it over them; and their great men exercise authority over them. But it is not this way among you, but whoever wishes to become great among you shall be your servant; and whoever wishes to be the first among you shall be slave of all. For even the Son of Man did not come to be served, but to serve, and to give His life a ransom for many (vv. 42–45).

The disciples saw leadership defined by control and influence. Jesus agreed that this is how the world views leadership, "But it is not this way among you." We do not shape our lives by the worldview(s) that govern our culture, but by the worldview of God. Our Lord sees true leadership in terms of servanthood not dominance.

Sadly, following the initial partaking of what we now call the Lord's Supper, on the very night Jesus was betrayed, we find the apostles in a repeat performance of their earlier visions of grandeur. Apparently while still at the table in the upper room, a dispute broke out concerning "which one of them was regarded to be the greatest" (Luke 22:24). Since they had learned nothing from Jesus' earlier instructions on this subject He repeats almost verbatim what He had told them as recorded in Mark 10:42–45 (Luke 22:25–26).

It seems to me that a careful study and application of what Jesus said to His self-centered apostles on these occasions would revolutionize our lives and our churches. At the very least we would begin to understand how it is that the Lord wants His people to serve one another. Individualistic Christianity, in which everybody becomes a world unto himself, is never on Jesus' radar. Nor do those who are jockeying for positions of prominence and authority please Him. The disciple of Christ is called to be one who has laid aside his own ambitions, who is following his Lord's commands, who is searching for ways to serve and who does so with a humble heart. Such people will not normally be recognized as great in the eyes of the unregenerate and often not in the eyes of Christians either. But to God, the only One who counts, they will be pleasing. As Paul said it this way,

"Therefore we also have as our ambition, whether at home or absent, to be pleasing to Him" (2 Corinthians 5:9).

The Body of Christ

In attempting to describe what the church is and how it is to function, the New Testament uses a number of metaphors. For example, the church is called a flock, a house, and a bride. But the most often used metaphor, and surely the most descriptive, is that of a body of which Christ is the head. First Corinthians 12 contains the most extensive use of this picture, building upon it an excellent understanding of how the church operates.

Much that is found in the first epistle to the Corinthians is in the form of a corrective. This first century local church was perhaps the most flawed of any church found in Scripture, although most of its theological understandings were accurate. Only their confusion in regard to the bodily resurrection was suspect and Paul addresses that issue in chapter 15. The Corinthians' problems were not doctrinal; they were applicational and personal. They had not allowed the truths of the Scriptures to change their behavior and in so many ways they still operated as if they were unregenerate. There was unchecked immorality in the church (chapter 5), lawsuits against fellow believers (chapter 6), misuse of the spiritual gifts (chapters 12–14), and much more. In chapter 12 a tangled mess of pride, selfishness, and dysfunctional behavior presents itself. Paul identifies the problem and exposes a wide spread misunderstanding and misappropriation of how God has set up the church. He does this through the metaphor of how the human body functions.

Members of the church at Corinth were apparently being arrogant and divisive concerning spiritual gifts. In regard to these sins Paul had much to say:

- All spiritual gifts are given to be used for the common good of the church (v. 7).

- All spiritual gifts are given according to the sovereign will of the Holy Spirit (vv. 11, 18, 27).

- All believers are members of the body and live to serve that body (v. 12).

- The Lord has sovereignly placed members in the body to serve as He has desired (vv. 14–16).

- Without such variety the body could not operate (v. 17).

- Each member of the body of Christ is dependent upon the other members (vv. 18–25).

- The body is designed so that its members are interconnected (v. 26).

- Specific gifts are given to the body so that it can properly serve the Lord, and each gift plays a unique part (vv. 27–31).

When we put all of this together we see clearly that God has designed and gifted His local assemblies so that we need one another, and the church cannot function as intended if we each do not live out the giftedness and divine placement in the body, according to His sovereign will and plan.

Having pastored at the same church for nearly four decades I have had ample opportunity to observe God's design for the local church in action. On the ugly side, I have seen people not gifted in administration frustrate themselves and their fellow believers when they take on, or are forced into, organizational roles they are not equipped to fulfill. I have seen people who lack the gift of teaching faithfully attempting to help others through providing formal instruction from the Word which they cannot articulate to anyone's satisfaction. I have seen men asked to take the position of elder, for which they were not qualified, only to watch them, and sometimes others, be harmed in the process. The list could go on. But happily, I have watched as numerous people over the years find the perfect spot for themselves in the body. I can tell when this has happened not only because the body is being edified, but because they joyfully serve. One of our church's missionaries, on home assignment and spending most of the year ministering among us, recently said they have never seen so many different people serve in a church and to do so happily. This comment was a source of great encouragement to me who, as a pastor, am often too close to the forest to see the trees. We recently had a banquet at our church and a couple of our young people volunteered to wash dishes. They washed from 5 to 9:30 pm. I came by and thanked them for their service to the Lord and one of the young men said, "Thank you for the privilege." The other one told me the next day that it was fun. These are choice high schoolers and I see them in much different roles in the years to come, partly due to the servant attitude that they exhibited that night.

What a joy it is to minister with people who serve with gladness of heart because they love the Lord, love people and are involved in the area of their giftedness and interests. But the body of Christ also provides accountability, protection and, when needed, correction. According to 1 Timothy 3:1–7 and Titus 1:5–9 churches are to be led by spiritually qualified and doctrinally sound elders. These men guard the flock from spiritual predators who would devastate God's people. Paul told the elders at Ephesus, "Be on your guard for yourselves and for all the flock, among which the Holy Spirit has made you overseers, to shepherd the church of God which He purchased with His own blood" (Acts 20:28). The elders guard the flock primarily by teaching sound doctrine and being willing and able to challenge those who teach error. As Paul wrote to Titus, "[Elders are] holding fast the faithful word which is in accordance with the teaching, so that [they] will be able both to exhort in sound doctrine and to refute those who contradict." Those not part of a biblically grounded fellowship are afforded no such protection. And those who are members of a church not led by such elders are far more susceptible to spiritual wolves. Churches with elders willing to fulfill their role as protectors are not always easy to find in an age when toleration of all things, even heresy, is viewed as a virtue. No one wants to be "negative" but the words found in Jude need to be given full weight,

> Beloved, while I was making every effort to write to you about our common salvation, I felt the necessity to write to you appealing that you contend earnestly for the faith which was once for all handed down to the saints. For certain persons have crept in unnoticed, those who were long beforehand marked out for this condemnation, ungodly persons who turn the grace of our God into licentiousness and deny our only Master and Lord, Jesus Christ (Jude 3–4).

In the process of bringing people into membership in our church, we ask if they are willing to place themselves under the authority of the elders of our congregation. We see this as important because God does. The inspired Scriptures command, "Obey your leaders and submit to them, for they keep watch over your souls as those who give an account" (Hebrews 13:17). This is not a power-play on the part of our

leadership, for we take seriously the exhortation found in
1 Peter 5:1–3:

> I exhort the elders among you, as your fellow elder and
> witness of the sufferings of Christ, and a partaker also of the
> glory that is to be revealed, shepherd the flock of God among
> you, exercising oversight not under compulsion, but voluntarily,
> according to the will of God; and not for sordid gain, but with
> eagerness; nor yet as lording it over those allotted to your
> charge, but proving to be examples to the flock.

This interaction within the body of Christ is important and
necessary on many levels, not the least of which is restoring
those ensnared by sin. Paul writes, "Brethren, even if anyone
is caught in any trespass, you who are spiritual, restore such
a one in a spirit of gentleness …" (Galatians 6:1). This can be
one of the most difficult, painful and messy things the church
of Christ attempts to do. Only love for Christ and people and
the desire to glorify the Lord will enable us to persevere at
times in such a task. But what a glorious task it is when a lost
sheep has been restored to Christ and the church has been
able to play a part in that restoration. For those outside the
fellowship, who have no one to care for their souls, the road
to renewal will be much more difficult. It is for reasons such
as these that every believer needs to be under the care not
only of Christ but of His church as well.

Conclusion

When it comes to fellowship within the body of Christ I consider myself to be among the most blessed people on earth. Through the entirety of my life I have had an almost uninterrupted experience of joy and encouragement with God's people. I grew up in an old fashioned fundamentalist church, the kind that has become the brunt of virtually everyone's jokes and anger today. Yet I have never known a people more kind, loving, sincere and genuine than that congregation. Today I might not agree with all their convictions and ways but they infected me with a love for Christ, Scripture and the church that has never left me. As a pastor, I have experienced the normal ups and downs of anyone in such a position. There have been deep valleys and occasional heartbreaks and sleepless nights. Yet, looking back, there is no other way that I would have chosen to live my life than by serving the body of Christ. Left to myself I am certain that my spiritual life would have become mutilated and distorted. I have needed God's people, their love, their rebukes, their encouragement, their short-comings, their ministry, their communion, to shape and direct me under the leadership of the Word and the Spirit. Spiritual growth and discipleship were intended by God to be forged in the crucible of the local church and its fellowship.

12

Biblical Discipleship—
The Transforming Life

Those knowledgeable with the biblical counseling movement, stemming from the ministry of Jay Adams, will be familiar with the put off/put on/renewal-of-the-mind principles relative to progressive sanctification. Drawn from a number of the epistles, especially Ephesians and Colossians, the teaching is that if people desire to change and grow spiritually they need to put off sinful behavior, replace that behavior with godly practices and foster new, biblical ways of thinking. This method, which is rooted in Scripture, seeks to aggressively and directly deal with sin, develop new habits that foster spiritual growth, and acquire a biblical mindset. In contrast, the approach taught within spiritual formation and contemplative spirituality looks to ancient, man-made disciplines and extra biblical experiences rather than the Word of God. In this chapter I want to explore the put off/put on/renewal-of-the-mind strategy common within the biblical counseling movement and recommend it as a most valuable means of discipleship.

In general, this approach teaches that when an individual seeks help dealing with actions, attitudes or thinking which has led to various levels of struggle, the counselor will begin by seeking to identify the problem. The difficulty at this point is that often the problem that is presented is not the real problem. For example, a couple may come seeking help because they are having difficulty getting along. They might be looking for some quick and simple techniques for improving their communication skills, or how to handle their finances more efficiently. And while these issues certainly need to be addressed, in the process of talking through all of this it becomes evident that the real problem is not that the couple spends too much or misunderstands each other, but rather it is because one is self-centered and the other is materialistic. The counselor could teach the couple a few communication principles and help them develop a budget, but this will only mask their real sin issues. If, in the process of counseling, this couple comes face-to-face with the reality of their spiritual condition and wants to change, what should they do? The counselor, if he or she is following the paradigm being described, will help this couple to first of all identify sins that are becoming evident. He or she will take them to the Bible and show them how to use it as a mirror to see their sins for what they are (James 1:23–25). They will then seek to "put off" those sins through the power of the Holy Spirit, obedience to Scripture, specific prayer, and the help of fellow believers. But it is never enough to merely attempt to stop sinful behavior; such behavior needs to be replaced by godly practices. Even then, without the renewing of their minds, including a major change in the way they think and process life, little will be accomplished. Put off/put on, without accompanying biblical thought patterns, is little more than psychological behaviorism. An unbeliever can put off a sinful habit and replace it with a healthy one and live a happier, healthier life. But these actions will not cause them to become more Christ-like. According to Romans 12:2, disciples should not be conformed to this world, but are to "be transformed by the renewing of [their] mind." A fundamental change in the way we think is necessary for spiritual transformation. Otherwise all that has been accomplished is external behavior modification which does not reach the heart. This is not spiritual transformation. Let's take a closer look below, first by examining two key New Testament texts.

Put Off/Put On/Renewal-of-the-Mind at Work

Ephesians 4:17–32

This portion of Scripture is essential in considering how believers change and grow spiritually. Not only is it full of great theological truth, but it is also extremely practical in nature. It begins with admonishing the child of God to no longer walk as the Gentiles walk, using Gentiles in this context to describe those who are not part of the people of God. A rather ugly description of those outside of the family of God follows: they walk in the futility of their mind; their understanding is darkened; they are excluded from the life of God because of their ignorance and hardness of heart; they have become callous so that they give themselves over to sensuality which leads them into every kind of impurity accompanied with greediness. This type of lifestyle is not how believers have been taught to live in the Scriptures (Ephesians 4:17–21).

At this juncture Paul reminds his readers what they have been taught: that their former life (described above) should be laid aside, along with the old self, or nature, that is corrupt and growing worse. They instead should be renewed in the spirit of their mind and put on the new self, a new nature formed in the likeness of God in all righteousness and holiness of the truth (Ephesians 4:22–24).

Having now described the put off/put on/renewing-of-the-mind principle, Paul now applies it to a number of practical situations (Ephesians 4:25–32):

Falsehood (v. 25): People lie for a number of reasons but mostly in order to deceive others to gain some sort of an advantage. Falsehood comes in many forms that are often ignored or excused such as exaggeration, flattery, spinning the truth, and hypocrisy, as well as blatant dishonesty. Since much of our world system operates deceitfully it is easy for believers to be caught up in the duplicity of our society. Scripture calls us to recognize falsehood, of any stripe, for what it is and lay it aside, replacing it with "speak[ing] the truth each one of you with his neighbor."

Anger (vv. 26–27): When we don't get what we want or think we need, it is natural for us to get angry, which may show up in the form of frustration, irritation, grumpiness, moodiness, as well as in more obvious forms. Prolonged anger gives the devil an opportunity to gain control of our lives and to ruin relationships as well as dishonor God. Rather than allowing anger to rule we are to make short work of it: "Do not let the sun go down on your anger." Paul returns to this subject of anger later in the passage (vv. 31–32) when he speaks of bitterness, wrath, clamor, slander and malice—all anger issues that need to be "put away." Anger must not be allowed to reign in our lives. It is to be replaced with a triad that is uncommon to our natural selves: kindness, tenderheartedness, and a forgiveness that follows the pattern of how God has forgiven us (v. 32).

Stealing (v. 28): Keeping in mind that Paul is writing to Christians, it is unlikely that many of them would be blatant thieves or robbers. But there are more subtle ways of stealing which are too often found among believers including: laziness on the job, an entitlement mentality in which one looks to others to do what we should do for ourselves; plagiarism, and even slander whereby we rob people of their good name. Here Paul calls on his audience to cease such activities and find work to not only care for their needs but to share with others. Theft, in any form, is not to be tolerated by disciples.

Unwholesome speech (vv. 29–30): Unwholesome is the idea of tearing down something. It is easy for us to harm people with our words, even without meaning to do so. We should endeavor to replace such speech with words that are edifying, or words that build up an individual. Our goal should be to dispense grace with our words rather than belittle or harm others. Verse 30 almost seems out of place in this list, but it is key to our understanding. It reads, "Do not grieve the Holy Spirit of God, by whom you were sealed for the day of redemption." It is the Holy Spirit that guides and empowers us to put off sinful behaviors and put on godly ones. When we resist Him we grieve Him, even though He has graciously sealed us so that nothing will ever rob us of our final redemption in the presence of God. It is the height of ingratitude and hardness to grieve the One who has done so much for us.

Colossians 3:5–17

The instructions found in Colossians parallel those in Ephesians, but here these principles are approached differently. In Colossians, Paul works from the basis of our position in Christ. In verse three he proclaims that believers "have died and [our] lives are hidden with Christ in God." The point Paul is driving home is that we are no longer slaves to sin; rather we have a new life grounded in the fact that we are now "in Christ." If we have died to that which has controlled us in the past and are now alive to the things of Christ, we should live out our position in Christ. This begins with "consider[ing] the members of [our] earthly body as dead to immorality, impurity, passion, evil desire, and greed" (v. 5). In addition we should put aside: "anger, wrath, malice, slander and abusive speech" and stop lying to one another (vv. 8–9). These sins, and others, should be replaced with "a heart of compassion, kindness, humility, gentleness, patience, bearing with one other," forgiveness, and love (vv. 12–14). The strength to live this way comes from the peace of Christ which is to rule in the believer's heart (v. 15), along with the word of Christ which is to richly dwell (to be at home) in our hearts (v. 16), as we do all things in the name of the Lord Jesus with gratefulness (v. 17). Paul is describing a radically transformed way of living that is to be the goal of every Christian. This is not a lifestyle reserved for a handful of "super saints." Progressively marching toward this type of godly living should be the norm among the people of God. This is what discipleship looks like.

Just as he does in the epistle to the Ephesians, in Colossians Paul applies these principles regarding practical life situations: marriage (3:18–21), work relationships (3:22–4:1), prayer life (4:2–4) and evangelism (4:5–6). Spirituality that does not have an impact on our everyday lives in major ways may have the appearance of piety but is not true discipleship as defined in Scripture.

Renewing of our Minds

Essential to our spiritual transformation, however, and without which no true change and growth is possible, is the renewing of our minds. When we become Christians we are made new creatures, "old things have passed away, behold, new things have come" (2 Corinthians 5:17). One of the new things that has come is a new mind. Our mind must be distinguished from our brain which will not be renewed until our final redemption (Romans 8:23). By coming to Christ our IQs do not necessarily increase; we don't go from being a "C" student to the top of the class; we don't suddenly develop reading skills we never possessed. What we do receive is a new capacity, through the regenerating power of the Holy Spirit, to see the glory of Christ (2 Corinthians 3:17; 4:6), understand the things of God (1 John 2:27), and discern and apply spiritual truth. First Corinthians 2:14–16 reads, "But the natural man does not accept the things of the Spirit of God, for they are foolishness to him; and he cannot understand them, because they are spiritually appraised. But he who is spiritual appraises all things, yet he himself is appraised by no one. For who has known the mind of the Lord that we should instruct Him? But we have the mind of Christ."

It is not enough, however, to have a new capacity to understand, appreciate and appropriate the things of God; our new mind needs to be informed. Since our minds do not come fully loaded with all theological and biblical truth and insight they must be trained in the ways of God. For this reason the Lord provides teachers to equip the body of Christ for ministry through systematic instruction in the Word (Ephesians 4:11–12; 2 Timothy 3:16–4:5). Personal study of the Scriptures is essential as well (2 Timothy 2:15; 1 Peter 2:2). In addition, individual discipleship provided by faithful believers to other faithful believers who will in turn disciple others is of vital importance and is the process described in the New Testament (2 Timothy 2:2; cf. Matthew 28:19–20).

With this in mind it is no surprise that sandwiched between the putting off various sins and the putting on godly virtues, in both the Ephesians and the Colossians texts we are informed of the need to be renewed in the way we think. In Colossians 3:10 Paul writes, "And have put on the new self who is being renewed in true knowledge according to the image of the One who created him." It is a bit clearer in Ephesians 4:23, "And that you be renewed in the spirit of your mind." To these passages must be added Romans 12:2 which reads, "And do not be conformed to this world, but be transformed by the renewing of your mind, so that you may prove what the will of God is, that which is good and acceptable and perfect."

The New Testament makes it abundantly clear that spiritual transformation takes place in the life of the believer as the believer's mind is renewed so that he/she is thinking increasingly more like Christ. This type of biblical thinking might not be as interesting to some or as trendy as adopting mystical techniques found in the Spiritual Formation Movement or various forms of mysticism. It might not seem as pious as asceticism or even monasticism. But it is the biblical methodology for developing true disciples of Christ. Anything else is purely human-created ideas layered upon the biblical paradigm.

Lest all of this is misunderstood to imply that our spiritual development is dependent solely upon our own efforts, it is important that we recognize that all spiritual growth is ultimately due to the indwelling presence and power of the Holy Spirit. Scripture, prayer and fellowship are means the Spirit uses, but it is the Spirit that empowers. Thomas Schreiner, in his biblical theology book *The King in His Beauty*, lays all of this out in such a marvelous way that I want to quote from him at length.

The coming of the Spirit represents the arrival of the power of the age to come during the present evil age. There is a close connection between the Spirit and power (Romans 15:13, 19; 1 Corinthians 2:4). Believers are empowered to live in a way that pleases God if they walk by the Spirit (Galatians 5:16; cf. Ephesians 3:16), are led by the Spirit (Romans 8:14; Galatians 5:18), march in step with the Spirit (Galatians 5:25), and sow to the Spirit (Galatians 6:8). Eschatological tension is evident, for the Spirit battles with the flesh (Galatians 5:17; cf. Romans 8:10), but the accent in Paul's theology is on the power of the Spirit to overcome sin, though sin persists until the day of redemption. There is a progressive change "from one degree of glory to another" from the Spirit (2 Corinthians 3:18). Those who are indwelt by the Spirit produce "the fruit of the Spirit" (Galatians 5:22–23; cf. Romans 8:5–6). Elsewhere Paul says that joy comes from the Holy Spirit (1 Thessalonians 1:6; cf. Romans 14:17), and that love is a work of the Spirit (Romans 15:30; Colossians 1:8). Believers are liberated from the power of sin and death through the Holy Spirit (Romans 8:2), so that those who have the Spirit fulfill "the requirement of the law" (Romans 8:4). They serve in a new way by virtue of the Holy Spirit (Romans 7:6), for "the letter kills, but the Spirit gives life" (2 Corinthians 3:6), and as a result those who are indwelt by the Spirit are given the freedom to obey (2 Corinthians 3:17). They slay by the Spirit "the deeds of the body" (Romans 8:13). Believers do what pleases God as they are filled with the Spirit (Ephesians 5:18), and the filling probably denotes both the Spirit as the means by which believers obey and the content with which believers are filled. The Spirit also enlightens believers so that they are able to grasp spiritual realities (1 Corinthians 2:10–16).[264]

The Holy Spirit's involvement in our lives and in our discipleship cannot be over-emphasized. Without His power we will hopelessly flounder in our efforts to live for the glory of God (cf. Ephesians 1:19–20; 3:14–21).

The Centrality of Christ

As we consider our spiritual maturation, and especially in relationship to the renewing of our minds, we need to note the centrality of Christ in the New Testament. As the inspired authors of Scripture shape our thinking through the truth of God's Word they repeatedly and consistently point us in the direction of Christ. Christian living is not mere behavioral modification and the Bible is not simply a how-to or self-help manual. What makes Christians different from all other people is the place of Christ in their lives.

Michael Horton warned, in his disturbing but penetrating book *Christless Christianity*, that evangelicalism has developed a form of Christian living virtually devoid of Christ. He begins his volume with an illustration from the ministry of Donald Grey Barnhouse, who was asked on his nationwide radio broadcast many years ago what things would look like if Satan really took control of a city. Barnhouse "speculated that if Satan took over Philadelphia, all the bars would be closed, pornography banished, and pristine streets would be filled with tidy pedestrians who smiled at each other. There would be no swearing. The children would say 'yes, sir' and 'no, ma'am,' and churches would be full every Sunday ... *where Christ is not preached.*[265]

This story well illustrates Horton's concern as he explains: "I think that the church in America today is so obsessed with being practical, relevant, helpful, successful, and perhaps even well-liked that it nearly mirrors the world itself. Aside from the packaging, there is nothing that cannot be found in most churches today that could not be satisfied by any number of secular programs and self-help groups."[266] This form of religion practiced by many Christians has been termed "moralistic therapeutic deism;" meaning faith is moralistic in that moral living is stressed, therapeutic in that it is guided by the desire to feel better about ourselves and deistic because God is not really necessary to the system. It is possible to live our Christian lives and create evangelical churches in which Christ is on the periphery and not central to belief and practice. But this is not true biblical Christianity that holds Christ as both preeminent and central.

This understanding of the faith is normative to church age teaching and the epistle to the Colossians is as good as any New Testament book to demonstrate this. Christ is referenced in this little letter of four chapters approximately 77 times and the whole epistle is wrapped around who Christ is and what He has done. Paul speaks of us being "in Christ" (e.g. 1:2, 28) and Christ being in us (e.g. 1:27); all things are created by Him, through Him, and for Him (1:28); we are buried with Christ and raised with Christ (2:12–13); we are to let the peace of Christ rule in our hearts and the word of Christ richly dwell within us (3:15–16). In Paul's understanding the believer has died and his life is hidden with Christ in God (3:3). As a matter of fact, perhaps the thesis of the epistle, which should be translated directly to our lives as Christians, is summed up perfectly in the next phrase, "When Christ, who is our life ..." (3:4). It is not theology as such or moral living in itself or spiritual experience or even eternal salvation. All of these things are vital, but it is Christ who is central; Christ who is our life. In Philippians 1:21 Paul writes, "For to me, to live is Christ and to die is gain." It is no wonder that the apostle determined to know nothing among those he ministered to "except Jesus Christ, and Him crucified" (1 Corinthians 2:2). And because Paul's theology is saturated with the crucified Christ it is not surprising that his message was brimming with Christ so that he could say, "But we preach Christ crucified," even though such a message was considered foolish to Gentiles and offensive to Jews (1 Corinthians 1:23). Why preach a foolish and offensive message? Because to the "called" it is the power of God and the wisdom of God (1 Corinthians 1:24). As the apostle wrote in Romans 1:16, "For I am not ashamed of the gospel, for it is the power of God for salvation to everyone who believes ..."

Returning to Colossians we can see how all this is fleshed out in the lives of those in the first century church. Paul begins by thanking God for what He has done in the believers' lives at Colossae as evidenced by their faith in Christ, love for the saints and hope laid up in heaven (1:1–8). Paul is not content, however, with the spiritual advancement of these Christians, urging them on to greater maturity in Christ (1:9–12). He wants to see them full of the knowledge of God's will, walking in a manner worthy of the Lord, pleasing Him in everything and being strengthened by the Lord's power. The believer needs to know that he has been rescued by Christ from the domain of darkness and transferred to the kingdom of God's beloved Son who has redeemed us and forgiven our sins (1:13–14).

In order to attain this level of life they first must understand the incomparable greatness of Christ which is detailed in 1:13–29. Here they are told both of the identity of the Lord Jesus—He the very image of God, firstborn of all creation— as well as His accomplishments. He is the eternal creator and sustainer of all things, head of His body the church, preeminent over all things, reconciler by means of His blood (1:15–23). In addition, Paul has been commissioned to reveal to the saints a mystery—something not previously known and knowable only through revelation from God. This mystery consists of Christ indwelling His people, both Jews and Gentiles, and drawing them into one body, the church (1:24–2:3).

Yet despite all that Christ is and has provided for His
children there is danger lurking ahead. The danger comes in
the form of false teachings that will seek to draw the saints
away from the centrality of Christ (2:4–23). In general the
concern is that the Colossian Christians will be deluded
by persuasive arguments (2:4–7). Those arguments come in
the form of philosophies and empty deceptions that stem
from human wisdom rather than Christ (2:9). At this point
Paul cannot resist turning once again to the excellencies of
Christ, as if by doing so the Colossians will see the massive
contrast between what is found in Christ and what is found
in these deceptive influences (2:9–15). For it is in Christ
that all the fullness of deity dwells in bodily form (v. 9); it
is in Christ that we have been made complete, as He is the
head over everything (v. 10); it is in Christ that our body of
flesh has been removed (v. 11); it is in Christ that we have
received spiritual baptism (v. 12); it is in Christ that we have
been forgiven (vv. 13–14); and it is in Christ that our spiritual
enemies have been defeated (v. 15). Having completed this
overview of what the believer has in Christ, Paul returns
to the dangers at hand. They come in three specific forms:
legalism (2:16–17), mysticism (2:18–19), and asceticism (2:20–
23). These are three philosophical/theological enemies that
seek to rob the saints of the life that is theirs in Christ.

In chapter three Paul turns his audience back to what
Christ-centered saints should be like. The disciple of Christ is
to seek Christ (3:1), set his mind on Christ (3:2), and live for

Christ (3:3–4). With this focus on Christ firmly embedded in their thinking, believers are now able to have a vibrant spiritual experience (which has already been described above) that honors and glorifies the name of Christ (3:17) and that translates to every avenue of their lives (3:18–4:6).

Conclusion:

Other forms of spirituality, both in biblical times as well as today, may have the appearance of "wisdom in self-made religion" (2:23), but in the end they are mere detours from the real life found in Christ. Like the Colossians, Paul was concerned that the Corinthian church was being led to a spiritual dead-end. He writes, "But I am afraid that, as the serpent deceived Eve by his craftiness, your minds will be led astray from the simplicity and purity of devotion to Christ" (2 Corinthians 11:3). Spiritual formation, mysticism, New Age spirituality and a host of other influences draw believers today away from the simplicity of Christ. Our Lord would have us cling tenaciously to Christ Himself, shedding the weights that slow us down and the sins that so easily entangle us, so that we can run the race set before us with endurance, "fixing our eyes on Jesus, the author and perfecter of faith" (Hebrews 12:1–2).

Conclusion
Roots of the Spiritual Formation Movement

Throughout this volume the Spiritual Formation Movement has been in the spotlight. And while we have examined the birth of the modern movement as well as its key beliefs, leaders and teachers, both past and present, we now want to turn our attention in this conclusion to the ancient roots. Coupled with this it would be of value to discuss the attraction of the movement, especially for evangelicals. Having already documented in previous chapters serious errors in doctrine and practice, why do so many evangelicals embrace the disciplines and look to the so-called "spiritual masters" for guidance? These issues of origin and attraction overlap but we will look at them separately for clarity's sake.

Roots

All trees are sustained by a root system and, while there are many roots of various sizes within the system, there is usually a main root or two from which other roots sprout. There are two ancient main roots of spiritual formation that need exploring: the theological root and the experiential root.

Theological roots

Even a casual reading of the New Testament reveals that the church, even in biblical times, struggled with doctrinal errors and heresies. Virtually all the epistles, with the possible exception of the short and personal letter to Philemon, addressed one or more theological concerns which run all the way from the person of Christ to the gospel message to abuse of gifts to eschatological confusion. There has been no perfect church or church age in which doctrinal inaccuracies cannot be found. But as the last of the apostles passed from the scene, by the end of the first century, theological blunders began to escalate both in number and in nature. Serious deviation, from apostolic teaching began to multiply throughout the church. I will detail a few of these below but first the cause of this heterodoxy needs identification, which I believe primarily to be the hermeneutical approach adopted by the earlier Church Fathers, beginning with Origen.

Origen (AD 185–254) rejected the single meaning of a text of Scripture and adopted the Greek allegorical approach popular in secular mythological literature especially in the Alexandria, Egypt, region in which he lived. Before him the Jewish scholar Philo had done the same with Old Testament Scripture and rabbinical literature. From this backdrop Origen popularized a view of biblical interpretation which taught that every passage of Scripture had various levels of meaning from the literal, which was the simplest, to the allegorical, which was the most profound and was considered the deeper and richer form of biblical interpretation. Origen, and those who accepted this hermeneutic, looked for hidden, symbolic meanings within the biblical texts, meanings that in actuality were not intended by the author. The net result was that, rather than attempting to understand what the Scriptures were actually saying, foreign ideas were being read into the passages. This method was guided by personal imagination instead of informed study which of course led to all sorts of fanciful and, at times, heretical, interpretations. Origen himself ultimately developed a number of recognized heresies such as universalism and the pre-existence of souls.

Perhaps Origen's most influential book, at least as far as interpretation of Scripture goes, was his *Commentary on the Song of Songs* in which his allegorical model was put on display. The groom in the Song was interpreted to be the Word of God and the bride as both the church of Christ and the individual soul. One author, who is supportive of

Origen's views, wrote, "Almost all Christian spiritual and ascetic literature, ever since, has been indebted to Origen's foundational architecture of Christian mysticism."[267]

Later the desert fathers followed in Origen's footsteps. Gerald Sittser wrote concerning this group,

> Their overall approach to the Bible seems—and, in fact, is— foreign to the modern age. They jumped from text to text, as if by free association, making connections that would appear odd to us, and they interpreted the Bible allegorically, which gives the impression that their interpretation is informed more by fanciful imagination than by careful exegesis.[268]

This approach to Scripture ultimately led to numerous schools of spirituality (ways of living out the gospel) such as Augustinian, Dominican, Benedictine, Ignatian and so forth. But ultimately they all had one thing in common, the so-called tripartite division of spiritual life. The *sine qua non* of this three-fold division consists of purgation, illumination and union and is found in all forms of mysticism, not just Christianized forms. Greg Peters defines these terms:

> The purgative way consists in one's active cleansing and is aided by spiritual exercises and ascetic practices, through the cultivation of humility and by practicing the virtues. Further advancement is made with the assistance of meditation, prayer and contemplation. The illuminative way is characterized by

further meditation, prayer and contemplation, combined with the reception of the gifts of the Holy Spirit, additional spiritual exercises and a devotion to the Virgin Mary. The unitive way involves the exercising of proper Christian love until one experiences, or achieves mystical union with God as Trinity.[269]

Said more simply, purgation is emptying oneself not only of sin but of passion, desire and even of intellectual thought. Illumination is what takes place when the Lord fills the emptiness of our souls and minds with extra-biblical knowledge and experiences and union is that mystical contact with God that cannot be rationally described, only experienced. This is the goal of all mystics, yet the three-fold way of spirituality is not found in Scripture. It is a mystical invention rooted in the errant theology of those who were foundational in what we are now calling spiritual formation.

Experiential Roots

During the first two centuries of church history persecution and martyrdom were not uncommon. The church stood against the corrupt world system and the devil and many Christians suffered as a result. The heroes of the faith were the martyrs who willingly made the ultimate sacrifice for Christ. With the legalization of Christianity in AD 312 by Constantine the cultural dynamics changed. But accompanying social and legal acceptability of the Christian faith was a watering down of dedication. The church was flooded with new "Christians," the majority of whom were

Christian in name only. And, with martyrdom a thing of the past, who would become the spiritual heroes of a new generation? Stepping into this void were the hermits and monks who later became known as the desert fathers and mothers. They originally moved to the deserts of Egypt, and similar areas because it was their belief that Satan still ruled there and they sought battle with him as Christians had battled him during times of persecution. And in face of a softening approach to the Christian life they wanted to demonstrate dedication. As their reputations grew, the desert fathers and mothers became the Christian heroes of their day. Many flooded to the deserts to see these living martyrs, to perhaps learn from them, and some to join them.

In misguided attempts to demonstrate and foster dedication these hermits and monks practiced extreme forms of asceticism including fasting, prolonged days without sleep, exposure to the elements, loneliness, celibacy and voluntary poverty. As time passed these practices became the badges of a select group of people called "spiritual athletes" and "bloodless martyrs." Their ascetic behavior became codified and imitated. It was under these extreme, self-induced physical conditions that some of the "spiritual athletes" began to claim visions and revelations from the Lord. These were passed down orally by their followers and then recorded in books to be spread throughout the Christian community. These writings became the basis for new forms of spiritualties that continue to have an impact on the church to this day.

Those in the Spiritual Formation Movement today look continually to this group, which they call spiritual masters and physicians of the soul, for insights into a deeper life with God. The roots of spiritual formation are planted in the desert fathers and mothers of the second to sixth century.

However to these early formers of mystical and ascetic spirituality must be added a number of others who mostly appeared in the Medieval Era, an era variously pegged as from 325 (the council of Nicaea) to 604 (the death of Pope Gregory the Great) and ending from 1453 (the fall of Constantinople to the Turks) to 1517 (Luther posting his "Ninety-Five Theses"). Developers and promoters of these forms of Christianity included Anselm of Canterbury (1033–1109), Bernard of Clairvaux (1090–1153), Bonaventure (1217–1274), Francis of Assisi (1181–1226), Dante Alighieri (1265–1321), Meister Eckhart (1260–1327), Pseudo-Dionysius (c. 500), and Thomas à Kempis (1380–1471), to name a few. Around the time of the Reformation a number of efforts were made by Rome to draw those who had adopted Reformational theology back to the Catholic Church. This Counter-Reformation was led in part by those who supported mystical and ascetic views and insights. This same group popularized their ideas by means of their own experiences, supposed visions and writings. St. John of the Cross, Teresa of Ávila, and Ignatius of Loyola (the founder of the Jesuits) were among the luminaries.

Julian of Norwich (1342–1416) is somewhat representative of this latter group. She was a nun in Norwich, England, who was locked in a cell that was attached to a church and lived there in seclusion (such women were called anchoresses). These cells or anchorholds would have a window that looked into the church so the individual could participate in the worship services. There would also be another window in which to receive food and water. While living in this condition, and at a time of extreme sickness, Julian claimed that she received 16 "showings" (revelations) on May 8, 1373, when she was 30 years old. These showings are held in high regard by the mystics and became somewhat of a pattern for the visions of others, which became increasingly common during this era.[270]

Consistent throughout the history of the mystical and ascetic spiritualties, including those promoting spiritual formation today, has been the four-fold hermeneutical approach to Scripture, attempting to follow the three stage pathway to spirituality (purgation, illumination, union), as well as openness to extra-biblical visions, revelations, traditions and practices. It is the acceptance of these three foundational premises that has enabled this branch of Christianity to survive and flourish.

Most evangelicals, one would think, would recognize these as obvious problems and turn away, yet so enamored are many with this approach to life with God that even relatively strong conservatives are willing to drop their safeguards and minimize the clear teaching of Scripture in order to glean from these mystics what they believe will be spiritual insights. This is true even as these evangelicals are aware that the theological foundation of this system of spirituality is often corrupt to the core. One of the most interesting and puzzling examples of this is Dr. Bruce Demarest, former professor of theology and spiritual formation at Denver Seminary for more than thirty years. Demarest is a man who has studied and taught evangelical theology for virtually his entire life and recognizes true heresy when he sees it. In writing the chapter "Reading Catholic Spirituality" in the book *Reading the Christian Spiritual Classics*, Demarest expresses deep appreciation for what he has learned from Roman Catholics concerning spiritual life. Yet he knows full well that the spiritual masters that he promotes and the teachings of Rome are in serious doctrinal error. He identifies a number of these himself: Catholic spiritual writers placed church tradition on a par with Scripture and used faulty hermeneutics; they believed in papal supremacy and infallibility; they had a low view of the fall and human sinfulness; they did not call clearly for conversion; they did not believe in justification by faith alone; they believed in a redemptive role for Mary; they prayed to Mary and the saints; they practiced severe asceticism; they promoted unbiblical mysticism; and they were, and are, a pathway to Eastern religions.[271] Fred Sanders, another author who is supportive of those many call the spiritual masters and their classics, nevertheless admits,

"These non-evangelical traditions may hold the gospel itself in stewardship, but they are messing it up, and a messed-up gospel is not the gospel; its result is dysangel, not evangel; bad news, not good."[272]

These are hardly negotiable doctrines that can be dismissed as unimportant. The positions taken by the "spiritual masters" and the Church of Rome place them outside the realm of biblical Christianity and demonstrate a clear rejection of the gospel. What kind of spirituality can be learned from those who almost certainly do not know Christ? Why are people drawn to a methodology of spirituality promoted by people who believe false doctrines and practice extreme and unbiblical forms of asceticism? What is the attraction?

Attraction

Bruce Demarest, mentioned above as a former theological professor at a conservative seminary, and one who knows that the doctrinal positions of the "spiritual masters" are deeply flawed to the point of presenting another gospel altogether, has nevertheless become a strong supporter of the spirituality drawn from these very people. Demarest's journey into the spiritual formation movement is similar to that of many. In his book *Satisfy Your Soul* he tells of his evangelical church sponsoring a 6-week course in the late 1980s on spiritual formation taught by a team from the Catholic Archdiocese of Denver. While he was resistant at first, he became interested in what was being taught and entered into a spiritual direction relationship for several years with the team leader. His director later convinced Demarest to attend workshops and retreats at a Benedictine renewal community in New Mexico. Eventually in 1995 he spent 6 weeks at the community in a residential program designed for spiritual direction. This seemed to break his final resistance to spiritual formation and upon returning to Denver Seminary he began developing graduate courses to teach what he had learned. This has not been an easy journey for Professor Demarest for, "Admittedly I found that certain beliefs and traditions remained foreign to me, being based more on tradition than solidly on Scripture ... But I also found that, once I got past my old prejudices and misunderstandings, I accepted more than I rejected."[273] This journey was so bewildering that even Ralph Martin, a well-known Roman Catholic scholar, wrote in the flyleaf, "What an amazing journey Bruce Demarest has been on. While remaining solidly rooted in his own evangelical tradition, he has, with great honesty and courage, opened himself to the deep and vital spiritual life in Christian history that has much to offer us today. This book will be profoundly enriching to the Christian who desires something 'more' in their union with God."[274]

As documented earlier Demarest is well aware of the doctrinal heresies and mutilated gospel that stems from the Roman Catholic Church and the creators of their ancient spirituality. But he seemed to "get over it" and accepted what good he could find while paying little attention to the bad.

He believes that the evangelical community has not balanced conversion of the soul with spiritual development of the soul and thus needs aid in understanding how to maintain such balance. For help, he claims, "We can turn to our Christian past—to men and women who understood how the soul finds satisfaction as we grow in God, and how His Spirit finds a more ready home in us."[275] He is sure that help can be found in this source because "spiritual formation is an ancient ministry of the church, concerned with the 'forming' or 'shaping' of a believer's character and actions into the likeness of Christ ... Many practices [were taught] that opened him or her to the presence and direction of God."[276]

Demarest was looking for something "more" in his Christian life and he believes he has found it in spiritual formation, which he sees as "a form of discipleship we are rediscovering today."[277] He is not alone. Carl Trueman, dean of Westminster Theological Seminary states, "I think the medieval mystics should form a staple of the literary diet of all thoughtful Christians."[278] And Jamin Goggin and Kyle Stobel assures us that, when Richard Foster launched the modern Spiritual Formation Movement within Protestantism in 1978 with his book *Celebration of Discipline*, he was not creating anything new but was merely "recovering a well-worn path of ancient wisdom that helped to define evangelicalism itself."[279] The evangelical promoters of spiritual formation warn of the need for discernment when reading the spiritual classics but promise great rewards to those who do. Their mantra is that "we should be open but cautious." Even when some of their heroes within spiritual formation drift so far as seeing no difference between Buddhism and Christianity (as was the case of the modern Catholic mystic Thomas Merton),[280] we have little to fear. On the contrary, Merton's case demonstrates that there is much to fear when we try to mix truth with error. Merton actually was quite consistent and took his views to their logical conclusions. He saw that Buddhism, a religion with little interest in theology or truth, offered the same mystical experiences that contemplative Christianity did. They both use similar methods including ascetic disciplines and traveling the three-fold path of purgation, illumination and union. In the end he came to the idea that since doctrine did not matter and only experience did, Buddhism and his understanding of Christianity were offering the same thing. He wanted something more and he found it. But that something is not biblical Christianity—since it does not meet the criteria God has handed down in His Word—and therefore it is false.

This is the danger facing everyone traveling down the spiritual formation corridor. In search of something more and being convinced by the many spiritual formation authors, past and present, that they are missing out on something, many are buying into the false teachings and false promises of spiritual formation. This journey, begun sincerely, will end badly for many.

A Final Word on the Disciplines

The Spiritual Formation Movement claims to offer an almost unlimited number of spiritual disciplines that will aid in forming Christian character. As I have tried to demonstrate throughout this book, while some of these have a bit of basis in Scripture, others have none, and even those which seem to be drawn at least in part from the Bible go beyond the Word in either their actual practice or what they promise or both. It is important to affirm that the word "discipline" is a good one and found in Scripture (e.g. Colossians 2:5). The issue is not whether discipline is helpful, even necessary, for spiritual development—it is, for self-control is one facet of the fruit of the Spirit (Galatians 5:23). Nor do I deny that there are specific disciplines that aid in progressive sanctification. At issue is what disciplines have actually been given to believers as a means of discipleship. It is my conviction that any means which the Lord has ordained for our use in the process of spiritual growth would be identified in the Scriptures. If the Bible is God's complete, authoritative revelation to us today, and if it is designed to make us "adequate, equipped for every good work" (2 Timothy 3:16–17), then we should have every confidence that the inspired text would include, with clarity, the instruments or means by which God would have us grow. We do not need to reach beyond the written Word to seek practices for spiritual development and intimacy with our Savior. The Lord is desirous that we know these things and has made no effort to hide them from us. It is not necessary for monks or hermits or other spiritual leaders from the past

(or present) to unearth some secret formulas designed to
teach us spiritual formation. All that we need to know on this
subject is found with certainty in God's divine revelation, the
Scriptures.

This does not mean that we cannot learn from fellow
believers; we surely can and must. For example in 2 Timothy
2:2 Paul instructs Timothy to take the things Paul had taught
him and teach them to other faithful men who in turn will
teach others. But what Timothy was to pass on was not
his own views and experiences and visions but the truth of
the Word of God given him by the inspired apostle (see
2 Timothy 1:13–14; 2:14; 3:10–4:5; Jude 17; Hebrews 2:3–4).
The early church gathered primarily to devote themselves to
the apostles' teaching (Acts 2:42), not to study the supposed
revelations of uninspired men and women. The body of Christ
is essential in our spiritual development (Ephesians 4:11–16)
and we aid that development as we "speak the truth in love"
to one another (Ephesians 4:15). We also help one another
with practical application of biblical truth. For example
in Titus 2, older women are instructed to "encourage the
young women to love their husbands, to love their children,
to be sensible, pure, workers at home, kind, being subject to
their own husbands, so that the Word of God will not be
dishonored" (vv. 3–5). It should be noted that what the older
women are to do by way of encouraging the younger women
is to facilitate appropriation of truth already revealed in
Scripture, not add ideas and revelations to Scripture.

When we turn to the Word of God to discover the Lord's clear teaching on discipleship what do we find? First, admittedly the Bible is a big book with many layers of wonderful truths about God, ourselves, redemption, the world, future events and more, waiting to be explored. It is a multi-faceted revelation from God that reveals the wonders of Christ "in whom are hidden all the treasures and wisdom of God" (Colossians 2:3). This leads to perhaps the primary distinction between the Spiritual Formation Movement and biblical discipleship. Both camps would claim Colossians 2:3 for themselves and both would agree that it is in Christ that all the treasures of wisdom and knowledge of God are hidden. The divide comes largely in the arena of revelation. Scripture promises believers divine power which will grant "us everything pertaining to life and godliness, through the true knowledge of Him [Christ] who called us by His own glory and excellence" (2 Peter 1:3). The question is, where is such knowledge of Christ found? Is it found in the Holy Scriptures or in extra-biblical revelations and dreams or both? As I argued in chapter seven I believe that the only inspired revelation from God for our times is the Bible. All other claims to revelations, however sincere or well-intended, lack the authority of Scripture. In addition, all other doctrines, methodologies, philosophies, traditions, and spiritual practices that do not emerge directly from the Word of God are at best suggestions and opinions, some helpful, others not and still others harmful. But when understood and proclaimed as having divine sanction these things fall under the condemnation of Jesus who warned the Pharisees that their traditions actually invalidate the Word of God (Mark 7:13). Similarly Paul warned the Colossians, "See to it that no one takes you captive through philosophy and empty deception, according to the tradition of men, according to the elementary principles of the world, rather than according to Christ" (Colossians 2:8). The Spiritual Formation Movement, as I have tried to demonstrate, has violated these principles and "are teaching as doctrines the precepts of men" (Mark 7:7). Rather than being deceived by the speculations of men may we "be diligent to present [our]selves approved to God as a workman who does not need to be ashamed, accurately handling the word of truth" (Colossians 2:15).

Endnotes

Chapter 1

1. James D. Maxwell III, http://www.faith.edu/resources/publications/faith-pulpit/message/the-new-spirituality/read

2. Desert Fathers and Mothers were hermits, ascetics, monks and nuns who lived in the desert of Egypt during the third and fourth century AD. There ascetic lifestyle was viewed as an alternative to martyrdom which previously has been seen as the highest possible sacrifice for the Lord

3. Bruce Demarest, *Satisfying Your Soul, Restoring the Heart of Christian Spirituality* (Colorado Springs: NavPress, 1999), p. 84.

4. Ibid.

5. Bruce Demarest, p. 23.

6. Richard J. Foster and Gayle D. Beebe, *Longing for God, Seven Paths of Christian Devotion* (Downers Grove: InterVarsity Press, 2009), p. 12.

7. Bruce Demarest, p. 26.

8. Ibid., p. 23.

9. Ibid., pp. 26–27, 34.

10. John Ortberg, *The Life You've Always Wanted, Spiritual Disciplines for Ordinary People* (Grand Rapids: Zondervan, 2002), p. 48.

11. Dallas Willard, *The Spirit of the Disciplines* (San Francisco: Harper, 1991), p. 95.

12. Ibid., p. 97.

13. Bruce Demarest, p. 35.

14. Dallas Willard, p. 99.

15. Ibid., p. 106.

16. Ibid., p. 101 (emphasis mine).

17. Ibid., p. 109.

18. http://blog.renovare.org/2003/05/20/heart-to-heart-on-christian-spiritual-formation/

19. As quoted in Demarest, p. 79.

20. John MacArthur, *Charismatic Chaos* (Grand Rapids: Zondervan, 1992), p. 65.

21. Demarest, p. 89.

Chapter 2

22. Donald Whitney, *Spiritual Disciplines for the Christian Life* (Colorado Springs: NavPress, 1991), p. 66.

23. Larry Crabb, *The PAPA Prayer, the Prayer You've Never Prayed* (Brentwood, TN: Integrity Publishers, 2006, p. 111.

24. Ibid., p. 143.

25. Richard Foster, *Celebration of Discipline* (New York: HarperCollins, 1998), p. 19.

26. Ibid., p. 25.

27. Ibid., p. 96.

28. Ibid., p. 166.

29. Ruth Haley Barton, *Sacred Rhythm* (Dowers Grove: InterVarsity Press, 2006), p. 68.

30. Ibid., p. 62.

31. Ibid., pp. 64–65 (emphasis hers).

32. Ibid., p. 71.

33. John Ortberg, *The Life You've Always Wanted, Spiritual Disciplines for Ordinary People* (Grand Rapids: Zondervan, 2002), p. 140.

34. Ibid., pp. 141–143.

35. Bruce Demarest, *Satisfying Your Soul, Restoring the Heart of Christian Spirituality* (Colorado Springs: NavPress, 1999), pp. 108–109.

36. Richard Foster, *Sanctuary of the Soul, Journey into Meditative Prayer* (Downers Grove: InterVarsity Press, 2011), p. 11.

37. Ibid., p. 13.

38. In all of the Old Testament fewer than 20 specific dreams to fewer than 15 people are recorded and only six in the New Testament. There are less than 25 visions to not more than 15 people in the Old Testament and even fewer in the New Testament. And none of these was ever given for mundane purposes (see *The Master's Seminary Jour*nal Vol. 22 #2, pp. 160–161).

39. Richard Foster, *Sanctuary of the Soul, Journey into Meditative Prayer,* p. 17.

40. Tricia McCary Rhodes, *Sacred Chaos, Spiritual Disciplines for the Life You Have* (Downers Grove: InterVarsity Press, 2008), p. 65.

41. Leighton Ford, *The Attentive Life, Discerning God's Presence in All Things* (Downers Grove: InterVarsity Press, 2008), p. 92.

42. Larry Crabb, p. 71.

43. Ibid., pp. 8, 13.

44. Cited in James Sundquist, *Who's Driving the Purpose Driven Church?* (Rock Salt Publishing, 2004), p.93.

45. Barton, *Sacred Rhythms,* p. 28.

46. Mark Yaconelli, *Downtime, Helping Teenagers Pray* (Grand Rapids: Zondervan, 2008), p. 74.

47. Barton, p. 76.

48. Richard Foster, *Sanctuary of the Soul, Journey into Meditative Prayer,* p. 28.

49. Cited in Ray Yunger, *A Time of Departing* (Silverton, Oregon: Lighthouse Trails, 2002), p. 84.

50. Richard Foster, *Sanctuary of the Soul, Journey into Meditative Prayer,* p. 15.

51. Ibid., p. 13.

52. Ibid., p. 18.

53.   Ibid.

54.   Ibid., p. 130.

55.   Ibid., pp. 62–88.

56.   Ibid., p. 71.

57.   Ibid., pp. 71–73.

58.   Ibid., p. 78.

59.   Ibid., pp. 80–88.

60.   Richard Foster and Gayle D. Beebe, "*Longing for God, Seven Paths of Christian Devotion* (Downers Grove: InterVarsity Press, 2009), p. 252.

61.   Bruce Demarest, p. 157 (emphasis mine).

62.   Leighton Ford, p. 77.

63.   Tricia McCary Rhodes, pp. 106–107.

64.   Ibid., p. 64.

65.   Ibid., p. 107.

66.   Mike King, *Presence-Centered Youth Ministry, Guiding Students into Spiritual Formation* (Downers Grove: InterVarsity Press, 2006), pp. 121–122.

67.   Ruth Haley Barton, *Strengthening the Soul of Your Leadership, Seeking God in the Crucible of Ministry* (Downer's Grove: InterVarsity Press, 2008), p. 64.

68.   Demarest, *Satisfy Your Soul*, pp. 269–277.

69.   Ibid., p. 276.

Chapter 3

70.   Bruce Demarest, *Satisfying Your Soul, Restoring the Heart of Christian Spirituality* (Colorado Springs: NavPress, 1999), p23.

71.   Ibid.

72.   Richard J. Foster and Gayle D. Beebe, *Longing for God, Seven Paths of Christian Devotion* (Downers Grove: InterVarsity Press, 2009), p. 15.

73.   Demarest, p. 23 (emphasis his).

74. Richard J. Foster with Kathryn A. Helmers, *Life with God, Reading the Bible for Spiritual Transformation* (New York: Harper One, 2008), p. 9.

75. Ibid.

76. Richard J. Foster and Gayle D. Beebe, *Longing for God, Seven Paths of Christian Devotion*, p. 134.

77. Ibid.

78. Richard J. Foster, *Sanctuary of the Soul, Journey into Meditative Prayer* (Downers Grove: InterVarsity Press, 2011), p.42.

79. As quoted in Richard J. Foster, *Sanctuary of the Soul, Journey into Meditative Prayer*, pp. 73–74.

80. Richard J. Foster, *Sanctuary of the Soul, Journey into Meditative Prayer, pp. 74–75*.

81. Ruth Haley Barton, *Sacred Rhythms, Arranging Our Lives for Spiritual Transformation* (Downers Grove, InterVarsity Press, 2006), pp. 54–55 (emphasis mine).

82. Leighton Ford, *The Attentive Life, Discerning God's Presence in All Things* (Downers Grove: InterVarsity Press), p. 93.

83. Richard J. Foster, *Sanctuary of the Soul, Journey into Meditative Prayer*, pp. 46–47.

84. Mike King, *Presence-Centered Youth Ministry, Guiding Students into Spiritual Formation* (Downers Grove: InterVarsity Press, 2006), p. 149.

85. The video can be viewed at:

86. Kenneth Boa, *Trinity: a Journal* (Colorado Springs: NavPress, 2001), p. 7.

87. Ibid., p. 8. Some trace the roots of the Spiritual Formation Movement to 1974 when Father William Menninger, a Trappist monk, found an ancient book entitled *The Cloud of Unknowing* in the library at St. Joseph's Abbey in Spencer, Massachusetts. This 14th century book offered a means by which contemplative practices, long used by Catholic monks, could be taught to lay people.

88. Kenneth Boa, *Historic Creeds: a Journal* (Colorado Springs: NavPress, 2000), p.10.

89. Ibid.

90. Kenneth Boa, *The Trinity: a Journal*, pp. 12–13.

91. Quoted in Richard Foster, *Celebration of Discipline, the Path to Spiritual Growth* (New York: HarperCollins, 1998), p. 206.

92. Richard Foster, *Life with God*, p. 64.

93. Bruce Demarest, p. 136.

94. Ibid., p. 139.

95. Mark Yaconelli, *Downtime, Helping Teenagers Pray* (Grand Rapids: Zondervan, 2008), pp. 113–114.

96. Ruth Haley Barton, *Sacred Rhythms*, p. 57 (emphasis mine).

97. Kenneth Boa, *The Trinity: a Journal*, p. 16.

98. Richard Foster, *Life with God*, p. 67.

99. Ruth Haley Barton, *Sacred Rhythms*, p. 57.

100. Mark Yaconelli, *Downtime*, pp. 117–119.

101. Kenneth Boa, *The Trinity: a Journal*, p. 19.

102. Richard Foster, *Life with God*, p. 68.

103. Kenneth Boa, *The Trinity: a Journal*, p. 19.

104. Tricia McCary Rhodes, *Sacred Chaos, Spiritual Disciplines for the Life You Have* (Downers Grove: InterVarsity Press, 2008), p. 70.

105. Kenneth Boa, *The Trinity: a Journal*, p. 20.

106. Ibid.

107. Ibid.

108. Quote in Bruce Demarest, p. 157 (emphasis mine).

109. Bruce Demarest, p. 138.

110. Quoted in Bruce Demarest, p. 96.

Chapter 4

111. Bruce Demarest, *Satisfying Your Soul, Restoring the Heart of Christian Spirituality* (Colorado Springs: NavPress, 1999), p. 128.

112. Ruth Haley Barton, *Invitation to Solitude and Silence* (Downer Grove: InterVarsity Press, 2010), p. 19.

113. Quoted in Ruth Haley Barton, *Invitation to Solitude and Silence*, p. 35.

114. Richard Foster, *Celebration of Discipline, the Path to Spiritual Growth* (New York: HarperCollins, 1998), p. 98.

115. Donald Whitney, *Spiritual Disciplines for the Christian Life* (Colorado Springs, NavPress, 1991), p. 184. In private correspondence to me Dr. Whitney clarified his position. He wrote, "Regarding silence and solitude, that's a chapter that will receive a great deal of revision when the book is revised. Please don't assume that I would still express things as written in 1991 … Basically I just want to argue that we do need times to be alone with the Lord, for the Scripture teaches this by example throughout. Furthermore, some disciplines, such as meditation on Scripture and personal prayer, seem to imply it. And with silence, essentially I am arguing that it is a corollary to times of being alone with the Lord, and that there are times where we need to "be silent before Him" as the prophets say. Before the Lord, I believe there's a time to be silent and a time to speak. I listen to Him speak through His Word (at which time my mouth usually needs to be shut) and I speak to Him through prayer and praise. Whatever those admonitions to "be silent before Him," is what I want to mean and teach. Rather than "turn inward," I want to shut my mouth sometimes in a *God-focused* silence."

116. Dallas Willard, *The Spirit of the Disciplines* (San Francisco: Harper, 1991), p. 160.

117. Quoted in Ruth Haley Barton, *Invitation to Solitude and Silence*, p. 12.

118. Quoted in Mark Yaconelli, *Downtime, Helping Teenagers Pray* (Grand Rapids: Zondervan, 2008), p. 134.

119. Ruth Haley Barton, *Sacred Rhythms* (Dowers Grove: InterVarsity Press, 2006), p. 32.

120. Quote in ibid., p. 29.

121. Ibid., p. 33.

122. Quoted in Richard Foster, *Celebration of Discipline, the Path to Spiritual Growth*, p. 96.

123. Richard Foster, *Celebration of Discipline, the Path to Spiritual Growth*, p. 102.

124. Ibid., p.102.

125. Ibid., pp. 102–103.

126. Ibid., p. 104.

127. Dallas Willard, p. 163.

128. Ibid.

129. Quoted in Bruce Demarest, p. 128.

130. Mark Yaconelli, *Downtime, Helping Teenagers Pray*, p. 56.

131. Ibid., p. 94.

132. Ibid., p. 96.

133. Richard Foster, *Celebration of Discipline, the Path to Spiritual Growth*, pp. 107–108.

134. Ibid., p. 108.

135. Ruth Haley Barton, *Invitation to Solitude and Silence*, p. 118 (cf. p. 101).

136. Ibid., p. 119.

137. Ibid., p. 122.

138. See ibid., pp. 72–74.

139. Ibid., p. 123.

140. Bruce Demarest, pp. 130–131.

141. Ibid., p. 131.

142. Ibid., p. 132.

143. Ruth Haley Barton, *Invitation to Solitude and Silence*, pp. 39–41.

144. Ibid., p. 41.

145. Jennifer Tafton, "Rediscovering Benedict," *Christians History and Biography*, Issue #93, p.6.

146. Ibid. p. 7.

147. Brian McLaren, *A Generous Orthodoxy* (Grand Rapids: Zondervan, 2004), p. 220.

Chapter 5

148. Mike King, *Presence-Centered Youth Ministry, Guiding Students into Spiritual Formation* (Downers Grove: InterVarsity Press, 2006), p. 39.

149. Dan Kimball, *The Emerging Church, Vintage Christianity for New Generations* (Grand Rapids: Zondervan, 2003), pp. 103, 115).

150. Quoted in Joan Chittister, *The Liturgical Year, the Spiraling Adventure of the Spiritual Life* (Nashville: Thomas Nelson, 2009), p. xiv.

151. Ibid., p. 16.

152. Ibid., pp. 21–22.

153. Robert Weber, *Ancient-Future Worship, Proclaiming and Enacting God's Narrative* (Grand Rapids: Baker Books, 2008), pp. 54–55.

154. Chittister, pp. 28–29.

155. Ibid., pp. 186–188.

156. Ibid., pp. 206–207.

157. Ibid., p. 100.

158. Ibid., p. 102.

159. Ibid., p. 103.

160. Ibid., pp. 105–106.

161. Ibid., pp. 202–203.

162. Robert Weber, *Ancient-Future Worship*, p. 74.

163. Ibid., p. 76.

164. Chittister, pp. 19, 64, 78, 102, 108–109, 135–136, 143–144, 159, 172, 186–188, 203–204.

165. Dan B. Allender, *Sabbath* (Nashville: Thomas Nelson, 2009), p. 5.

166. Ibid., pp. 27–28.

167. Ibid., p. 83.

168. Ibid., pp. 43, 61, 97, 120–130, 160–161.

169. Ibid., p. 47.

170. Ibid., p. 108 (see also pp. 110–111, 130–131).

171. Ibid., p. 110

172. Ibid., pp. 110–111.

173. Ibid., p. 125.

174. Ibid., p. 132.

175. Ibid., p. 156.

176. See Ibid., pp. 106, 112, 141, 146, 151–152,

177. Dan Kimball, p. 127.

178. Ibid., p. 128.

179. Mike King, p. 38.

180. Richard Foster , *Sanctuary of the Soul, Journey into Meditative Prayer* (Downers Grove: InterVarsity Press, 2011) pp. 40–41.

181. Ibid., p. 41.

182. Mike King, p. 133.

Chapter 6

183. http://www.nwjesuits.org/JesuitSpirituality/SpiritualExercises.html

184. http://en.wikipedia.org/wiki/Spiritual_Exercises_of_Ignatius_of_Loyola

185. Ignatius of Loyola (trans by Father Elder Mullan, 1914), *Spiritual Exercises of St. Ignatius of Loyola*, electric version location 283 of 3624.

186. Ibid., location 3165–3237.

187. James Wakefield, *Sacred Listening, Discovering the Spiritual Exercises of Ignatius Loyola* (Grand Rapids: Baker Books, 2006), p. 13 (emphasis his).

188. Leighton Ford, *The Attentive Life, Discerning God's Presence in All Things* (Downers Grove, InterVarsity Press, 2008), p. 197.

189. Richard Foster, *Life with God, Reading the Bible for Spiritual Transformation* (New York: Harper One, 2008) pp. 15, 66. See also Foster's *Celebration of Discipline, the Path to Spiritual Growth* (New York: Harper One, 1998) p. 29.

190. Bruce Demarest, *Satisfy Your Soul, Restoring the Heart of Christian Spirituality* (Colorado Springs: NavPress, 1999), p. 146 (emphasis his).

191. Mark Yaconelli, *Downtime, Helping Teenagers Pray* (Grand Rapids: Zondervan, 2008), p. 148.

192. Mike King, *Presence-Centered Youth Ministry, Guiding Students into Spiritual Formation* (Downers Grove: InterVarsity Press, 2006), pp. 183–185.

193. Gregory A. Boyd's endorsement of Wakefield's *Sacred Listening*.

194. Eugene Peterson's endorsement of Wakefield's *Sacred Listening* (emphasis his).

195. Ruth Haley Barton, *Sacred Rhythms, Arranging Our Lives for Spiritual Transformation* (Downers Grove, InterVarsity, 2006), p. 111(emphasis hers).

196. See James Wakefield, p. 7.

197. James Wakefield, pp. 8–9.

198. Ibid,. p. 13.

199. Ibid., p. 56.

200. Ibid., p. 91.

201. Location 884–899.

202. Ibid., p. 18, and location 331 in electronic version.

203. Ibid., p. 97.

204. Ibid., p. 162

205. Ibid., p. 25 (see also pp. 33, 37, 39, 45).

206. Ibid., p. 24.

207. Ibid., pp. 177–182.

Chapter 7

208. Adele Ahleberg Calhoun, *Spiritual Disciplines Handbook, Practices That Transform Us* (Downer Grove: InterVarsity Press, 2005), p. 99 (emphasis mine).

209. Ruth Haley Barton, *Sacred Rhythms, Arranging Our Lives for Spiritual Transformation* (Downers Grove: InterVarsity Press, 2006), p. 111.

210. Larry Crabb, *The Papa Prayer, the Prayer You've Never Prayed* (Brentwood, TN: Integrity Publisher, 2006), p. 8.

211. John Ortberg, *The Life You've Always Wanted, Spiritual Disciplines for Ordinary People* (Grand Rapids: Zondervan, 2002), p. 140.

212. Tommy Tenney, *The God Chasers* (Shippensburg, Pa: Destiny Image, 2000), unnumbered pages in introduction (emphasis his).

213. Dallas Willard, *Hearing God, Developing a Conversational Relationship With God* (Downers Grove, IL: InterVarsity Press, 2012), pp. 12, 13.

214. Ibid., pp. 26, 31, 67.

215. Ibid., p. 15.

216. Henry and Richard Blackaby, *Hearing God's Voice* (Nashville: Broadman & Holman Publishers), 2002, p. 234.

217. Ibid., p. 235.

218. Ibid., p. 236.

219. See www.desiringgod.org/blog/posts/piper-on-prophecy-and-tongues which reveals Piper's openness to modern prophecies even though this one proved to be false.

220. Mark and Grace Driscoll, *Real Marriage, the Truth about Sex, Friendship and Life Together* (Nashville: Thomas Nelson, 2012), p. 8. For more of Mark Driscoll's claims of extrabiblical revelations see his book *Confessions of a Reformission Rev, Hard Lesson from an Emerging Missional Church* (Grand Rapids: Zondervan, 2006), pp. 39, 74–75, 97, 99, 128, 130. See also, a five minute video clip in which Driscoll claims that God gives him revelations concerning the personal, intimate lives of people: http://teampyro.blogspot.com/2011/08/pornographic-divination.html

221. Matt Chandler, *The Explicit Gospel* (Wheaton: Crossway, 2012), p. 30.

222. Mark Galli, "The Mystic Baptist," *Christianity Today*, Nov 2012, p. 54.

223. Sarah Young, *Jesus Calling, Enjoying Peace in His Presence* (Nashville: Thomas Nelson, 2004), p. xii.

224. *The Westminster Confession*, chapter 1, section 6.

225. Quoted from Beth Moore's DVD "Believing God."

226. Wayne Grudem, *The Gift of Prophecy in the New Testament and Today* (Wheaton: Crossway, 1988), p. 14.

227. Ibid., p. 110.

228. Ibid., p. 120.

229. Ibid., pp. 120, 121 (emphasis mine).

230. Dallas Willard, p. 9 (emphasis mine).

231. As transcribed in John MacArthur, *Strange Fire* (Nashville: Thomas Nelson, 2013), pp. 241–242. The interview can be viewed at www.desiringgod.org/blog/posts/piper-on-prophecy-and-tongues.

232. Wayne Grudem., p. iii.

Chapter 8

233. Dallas Willard, *The Spirit of the Disciplines* (New York, HarperCollins, 1988), p. 167.

234. Ibid.

235. Ibid, emphasis his.

236. Richard Foster, *Celebration of Discipline* (New York: HarperCollins, 1998), p. 51.

237. Scot McKnight, *Fasting* (Nashville: Thomas Nelson, 2009), p. 155.

238. Ibid., pp. 32, 48, 70, 87, 110, 139, 152, xvii, 154, 155.

239. Ibid., pp. 20, 122.

240. Ibid., p. 97.

241. Ibid., p. 55.

242. John Piper, *A Hunger for God, Desiring God through Fasting and Prayer* (Wheaton: Crossway, 1997), pp. 185–186.

243. Ibid., p. 191.

244. Ibid., p. 35.

245. Ibid., p. 25.

246. Ibid.

247. Ibid., pp. 9–11.

248. Ibid., pp. 26–36.

249. Ibid., pp. 34–36.

250. Ibid., p. 37.

251. Ibid., pp. 19, 58, 202–204.

252. Ibid., p. 210.

253. Ibid., p. 106.

254. Ibid., p. 208.

255. http://www.christianitytoday.com/ct/2009/January/26.29.html

256. http://en.wikipedia.org/wiki/Spiritual_direction

257. Richard Foster, *Celebration of Disciplines* (New York: HarperCollins, 1998), p. 185.

258. Ibid.

259. William A. Barry and William J. Connolly, *The Practice of Spiritual Direction* (Harper & Row, 1986)

260. http://www.ignatianspirituality.com/making-good-decisions/spiritual-direction/

261. Kenneth Boa, *The Trinity, a Journal* (Colorado Springs: NavPress, 2001), pp. 22–23.

Chapter 11

262. William D. Mounce, Gen. Ed., *Complete Expository Dictionary of Old and New Testament Words* (Grand Rapids: Zondervan, 2006), p. 247.

263. Carl F. George, *Prepare Your Church for the Future* (Tarrytown: Revell, 1991), 129–131. http://app.razorplanet.com/acct/40309-3627/resources/59one_another_scriptures.pdf

Chapter 12

264. Thomas R. Schreiner, *The King in His Beauty, a Biblical Theology of the Old and New Testaments* (Grand Rapids: Baker Academic: 2013), p. 557.

265. Michael Horton, *Christless Christianity, the Alternative Gospel of the American Church* (Grand Rapids: Baker Books, 2008), p. 15 (emphasis his).

266. Ibid., pp. 16–17.

Conclusion

267. Louis Bouyer as quoted by Michael Glerup, "The Church Fathers and Mothers." *Reading the Christian Spiritual Classics, a Guide for Evangelicals*, ed. Jamin Goggin and Kyle Strobel (Downers Grove: InterVarsity Press Academic, 2013), p. 177.

268. Gerald L. Sittser, "The Desert Fathers," ibid., p. 199.

269. Greg Peters, "Spiritual Theology," ibid, p. 82 (cf. pp. 188–189).

270. For a fuller account see Greg Peters, "Medieval Traditions," ibid., pp. 240–242.

271. Bruce Demarest, "Reading Catholic Spirituality," ibid., pp. 120–128.

272. Fred Sanders, "Reading Spiritual Classics as Evangelical Protestants," ibid., p. 157.

273. Bruce Demarest, *Satisfy Your Soul: Restoring the Heart of Christian Spirituality* (Colorado Springs: NavPress, 1999), p. 35.

274. Ibid., flyleaf.

275. Ibid., p. 23.

276. Ibid., pp. 23–24.

277. Ibid., p. 23.

278. As found in *Reading the Christian Spiritual Classics, a Guide for Evangelicals*, p. 9.

279. Ibid., pp. 10–11.

280. See Demarest, *Satisfy Your Soul*, pp. 274–277.

Dr. Gary Gilley has been pastoring at Southern View Chapel in Springfield, Illinois, since 1975. He is author of five books, *This Little Church Went to Market, This Little Church Stayed Home, "I Just Wanted More Land," —Jabez, "Is That You Lord?"* and *This Little Church Had None.* He has also contributed to five other books, *Reforming or Conforming, Biblical Sufficiency Applied, Practical Aspects of Pastoral Theology, Dispensationalism Tomorrow & Beyond, a Tribute to Charles Ryrie,* and *An Introduction to the New Covenant.* Pastor Gilley is a frequent speaker at Bible conferences in America and internationally. He also writes the study paper, Think on These Things which examines important contemporary theological issues and trends. He is a board member of Brazil Gospel Fellowship Mission and the Personal Freedom Outreach, serves on the Board of Reference for New Tribes Missions and is the Book Review Editor for the Journal of Dispensational Theology. In addition he is married (Marsha) has two sons (Ben and Brian) and five grandchildren.